Editor's Note

As I was working on this year's almanac in the spring of 2022, highly contagious COVID variants were seeking out those few of us yet to be infected, Broadway shows were shutting down, and the subway seemed in peril. Some things were looking up—namely, rents, crime, the rat population, and the price of nearly everything. In May, the *New Yorker* cartoonist Colin Tom pretty much summed it up: Two women, sipping wine in a streetery somewhere near Canal Street. "It's just New York," one says. The other responds, "We all suffer."

And yet. On Instagram, New York Nico was still finding people goofily dancing in city parks and rooftops, and artist Devon Rodriguez was surprising straphangers with beautiful hand-drawn portraits of themselves—masks and all. New Yorkers celebrated the unofficial cannabis holiday 4/20 with abandon in Washington Square Park. And *New York* magazine was documenting stylish, over-the-top New Yorkers everywhere from an NYPD boxing match to a Staten Island shipping dock.

And, just like last year, I was amazed by the creativity, beauty, and playfulness of the concerts, festivals, exhibitions, and other events lined up for the coming year. I was able to include just a fraction of what will happen in 2023. Keep your eyes open for newly announced concerts and restaurant openings (even a long-rumored Manhattan Wegmans, and hopefully the completion of the Studio Museum's renovation)—and your pencil posed to record them here. Don't forget to check with each institution before you head out, since dates are subject to change. Mayor Adams keeps insisting that "New York is back, baby," but New Yorkers know it was never really gone. Now that I think about it, no wonder rents are up.

The Five-Borough Fashion Forecast: If trends continue on their same trajectory, we can expect 2023 to bring an increase in socially conscious dressing, with sustainably sourced fashion at the forefront. The growth of the vintage and secondhand markets points to the resurgence of past styles, while the vogue for thrifting ensures eclecticism in the urban fashion landscape. Still, rising inflation all but guarantees the persistence of fast fashion as a practical style solution during uncertain economic times. The booming luxury resale division, however, indicates that the mixing of high and low will be the order of the day. Also forecasted is the continuation of high-profile collaborations between fashion brands at different consumer levels.

Already a growing sector of the retail landscape, gender-neutral clothing will become more visible and readily available to the urban shopper. Whether browsing a boutique or visiting a Fifth Avenue mainstay, expect less emphasis on body-conscious designs and a greater focus on color, pattern, and surface decoration that transcend the gender binary. Also anticipate a more modular approach to assembling looks—with fewer coordinated ensembles and more mix-and-match pieces that encourage the cultivation of individual taste.

As the TikTok generation continues to chase fleeting microtrends more suited to social media than the city streets, a return to the classics is in order for the modern New Yorker. Time-honored staples take center stage; yet, we can anticipate a renewed interest in bold accessories to enliven otherwise understated ensembles. Capsule wardrobes and resort wear will make a grand return as international borders open, and urban dwellers resume their rigorous travel schedules.

Even as the post-pandemic world inches closer to normality, nostalgia for the pre-pandemic days will persist, as seen with the perpetuation of throwback trends like the "Y2K aesthetic." It seems that the cropped tees and low-rise jeans of the early 2000s will remain relevant for some time yet. As the fashion cycle continues to accelerate at a breakneck pace—forcing the revival of styles from increasingly recent eras—it is left to be seen whether fashion will keep drawing on its own past, or forge a new path forward.

JANUARY

NEW YORKERS COULD BE FORGIVEN if their New Year hangovers are severer this year. With the past two holiday seasons tamped down by the pandemic, New Yorkers might cut a little extra loose this New Year's Eve. Maybe *this* is the year to stick it out shoulder to shoulder with the tourists in freezing-cold temperatures, without food or water or bathrooms, unable to leave, or move, wearing branded felt top hats and goofy 2023 glasses for several hours before a pop star takes to the stage ... or maybe not. If you survive New Year's Eve, you can explore the Jewish experience through cinema at the **New York Jewish Film Festival and** celebrate the **Lunar New Year** at the annual Chinatown Parade or the **Chinese Documentary Film Festival** at Flushing Town Hall. Catch cutting-edge performances during the **Public Theater's Under the Radar Festival** and see Grammy winner **Rhiannon Giddens at Carnegie Hall**.

PROFESSOR VATICINATE SAYS, *on New Year's Day, it's wet you'll get. From the 4th to the 19th, expect frequent flakes; you're going to need snowblowers and nose blowers. Take a break before the big freeze and break out your skis! For the rest of the month, it will turn frigidly cold. Numb's the word.*

NORMALS FOR
CENTRAL PARK
Avg. high: 39.5°
Avg. low: 27.9°
Avg. rainfall: 3.64"
Avg. snowfall: 8.8"

The last time the temperature in NYC fell below zero was on Valentine's Day 2016, when the mercury dipped to -1°. The greatest number of consecutive below-zero days is four, from December 29, 1917, to New Year's Day 1918. The coldest temperature recorded at Central Park is -15° on February 9, 1934.

January is the cloudiest month: 14 days average more than 8/10 cloud cover.

Sky Watch: At the start of the year, four of the five naked-eye planets are visible in our early evening sky. Low in the west-southwest are dazzling Venus and a much-dimmer Saturn. These two planets will appear very close together on the 22nd. A crescent Moon sits to the upper left of these planets on the 23rd. Much higher in the southwest sky is brilliant Jupiter, while well up in the eastern sky is yellow-orange Mars.

ANNALS OF THE NIGHT SKY

It may come as a surprise for you to learn that at this coldest time of the year, Earth will actually arrive at its closest point to the Sun at 11 a.m. on the 4th, at a distance of 91,403,073 miles. And we're 3.1 million miles farther from the Sun on July 6. The 23½-degree tilt of Earth's axis is responsible for controlling our four seasons and not our ever-changing distance from the Sun.

NYC BOOK OF THE MONTH
The Age of Innocence by Edith Wharton (1920)

"On a January evening in the early seventies, Christine Nilsson was singing in Faust at the Academy of Music in New York." So begins Wharton's novel of social mores and sublimated desire set in the stifling upper-class milieu of the author's childhood. Newland Archer spies Ellen Olenska in an opposite box, and, within pages, she turns his world upside down.

NYC MOVIE OF THE MONTH
Midnight Cowboy, directed by John Schlesinger, starring Dustin Hoffman and Jon Voight (1969)

The only X-rated film to win an Oscar for best picture, *Midnight Cowboy* follows the unlikely bond formed between Joe, a would-be gigolo from Texas, and Ratso Rizzo, a city con artist. In one scene they dream of Florida, dancing awkwardly to "Orange Juice on Ice" in Rizzo's freezing squat—a set built from pieces of a condemned tenement.

January has 31 days.

Dec. 26–Jan. 1

"We are all, always, both urban anthropologist and subject of another stranger's fascination; the people-watcher and someone worth watching. This city wouldn't be the same without us."
—*New York* magazine, 2019

---

26 MONDAY
☼ 7:18 AM / 4:34 PM

Hanukkah ends.

Kwanzaa begins.

Metropolitan Opera presents Mozart's *Magic Flute* (and Dec. 28, 30).

---

27 TUESDAY
☼ 7:19 AM / 4:35 PM

Suzanne Vega: Home for the Holidays at City Winery Main Stage (and Dec. 22, 23, 26)

---

28 WEDNESDAY
☼ 7:19 AM / 4:36 PM

Feinstein's/54 Below presents the Ilene Graff Holiday Show.

---

29 THURSDAY
☼ 7:19 AM / 4:36 PM   ☽ 1ST QUARTER

New York City Ballet presents Balanchine's *Nutcracker* (through Dec. 31).

---

30 FRIDAY
☼ 7:19 AM / 4:37 PM

Gov't Mule plays the Beacon Theater (and 31st).

---

31 SATURDAY
☼ 7:19 AM / 4:38 PM

New Year's Eve

Times Square Ball Drop

New York Road Runners Midnight Run

---

1 SUNDAY
☼ 7:20 AM / 4:39 PM

New Year's Day • Kwanzaa ends.

Last chance to see *Wolfgang Tillmans: To look without fear* at the Museum of Modern Art

Jan. 2–8

"Basically, I wake up in the morning and I think everything's going to be great.... I pick up the *New York Times* and realize once again I'm wrong."

—Lewis Black

---

2 MONDAY

☼ 7:20 AM / 4:40 PM

Last chance to see *Barbara Kruger: Thinking of ~~You~~. I Mean ~~Me~~. I Mean You.* at the Museum of Modern Art

---

3 TUESDAY

☼ 7:20 AM / 4:40 PM

1870: Work begins on the Brooklyn tower of the Brooklyn Bridge.

---

4 WEDNESDAY

☼ 7:20 AM / 4:41 PM

The Public Theater's Under the Radar Festival kicks off (through January 22).

---

5 THURSDAY

☼ 7:20 AM / 4:42 PM   ●

Yuja Wang performs the New York Premiere of the Third Piano Concerto by Magnus Lindberg at David Geffen Hall, Lincoln Center (through Jan. 10).

---

6 FRIDAY

☼ 7:20 AM / 4:43 PM   ○ FULL MOON

Epiphany

Celebrate Three Kings Day at El Museo del Barrio.

---

7 SATURDAY

☼ 7:20 AM / 4:44 PM

Orthodox Christmas Day

1943: Nikola Tesla dies on the 33rd floor of the Hotel New Yorker.

---

8 SUNDAY

☼ 7:20 AM / 4:45 PM

Last chance to see *New York: 1962–1964* at the Jewish Museum

Jan. 9–15

"New York is the perfect model of a city, not the model of a perfect city."
—Lewis Mumford

9 MONDAY
☼ 7:19 AM / 4:46 PM

1854: Jennie Jerome, "dollar princess" and mother of Winston Churchill, is born in Brooklyn.

10 TUESDAY
☼ 7:19 AM / 4:47 PM

Metropolitan Opera presents Gaetano Donizetti's *L'Elisir d'Amore* (through Apr. 29).

11 WEDNESDAY
☼ 7:19 AM / 4:48 PM

1886: New Yorker William Steinitz wins the first game of the first-ever Chess World Championship at Cartier's at 80 Fifth Avenue.

12 THURSDAY
☼ 7:19 AM / 4:49 PM

Wallis Bird plays Rockwood Music Hall.

13 FRIDAY
☼ 7:18 AM / 4:50 PM

NYC Winter Jazzfest Marathon (and 14th)

14 SATURDAY
☼ 7:18 AM / 4:52 PM ☾ 3RD QUARTER

Musical Explorers Family at Carnegie Hall

15 SUNDAY
☼ 7:17 AM / 4:53 PM

Metropolitan Opera presents Francis Poulenc's *Dialogues des Carmelites* (through Jan. 28).

Jan. 16–22

"When I finally got here, I was like, 'Wait, you mean this city is actually real?'... Everyone who drove a cab was writing a novel. Every waitress was a dancer."
—Eileen Myles

16 MONDAY

☼ 7:17 AM / 4:54 PM

"Living Lantern" winter art installation opens on the Garment District pedestrian plazas (through Feb. 24).

17 TUESDAY

☼ 7:17 AM / 4:55 PM

Martin Luther King Jr. Day

New York City Ballet presents All Balanchine (and Jan. 18, 19, 21, 25, and 28).

18 WEDNESDAY

☼ 7:16 AM / 4:57 PM ♓ PISCES

The Cleveland Orchestra plays Carnegie Hall.

19 THURSDAY

☼ 7:16 AM / 4:57 PM

yMusic plays Zankel Hall Center Stage at Carnegie Hall.

20 FRIDAY

☼ 7:15 AM / 4:58 PM ♒ AQUARIUS

The Winter Show (an art, antiques, and design fair) opens at 660 Madison Ave. (through Jan. 29).

21 SATURDAY

☼ 7:14 AM / 5:00 PM ● NEW MOON

Claire Chase plays *Pauline Oliveros at 90*, Zankel Hall Center Stage at Carnegie Hall.

22 SUNDAY

☼ 7:14 AM / 5:01 PM

Lunar New Year

Giuseppe Bausilio plays Feinstein's/54 Below.

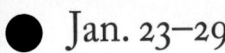

Jan. 23–29

"To think of 'living' there was to reduce the miraculous to the mundane; one does not 'live' at Xanadu."
—Joan Didion

23 MONDAY
☼ 7:13 AM / 5:02 PM

The MET Orchestra Chamber Ensemble plays Weill Recital Hall at Carnegie Hall.

24 TUESDAY
☼ 7:12 AM / 5:03 PM

Rhiannon Giddens with Francesco Turrisi: They're Calling Me Home, at Zankel Hall at Carnegie Hall

25 WEDNESDAY
☼ 7:12 AM / 5:04 PM

1915: First transcontinental telephone call between San Francisco and New York

26 THURSDAY
☼ 7:11 AM / 5:06 PM

Roundabout Theatre Company presents *The Wanderers* by Anna Ziegler at the Laura Pels Theatre in the Harold & Miriam Steinberg Center for Theatre.

27 FRIDAY
☼ 7:10 AM / 5:07 PM

World Holocaust Victims Remembrance Day

Brian Letendre plays Feinstein's/54 Below.

28 SATURDAY
☼ 7:09 AM / 5:08 PM   ☾ 1ST QUARTER

Young People's Concert: Dance Like a Firebird at David Geffen Hall, Lincoln Center

29 SUNDAY
☼ 7:08 AM / 5:09 PM

Juan Diego Flórez, tenor, and Vincenzo Scalera, piano, play Stern Auditorium/Perelman Stage, Carnegie Hall.

FEBRUARY

Februarys cold winter wind seeps into the window cracks of high-rises and prewar buildings and the gap between the scarf and your coat collar. When the winter blues start to seep in, too, taking a turn on the ice might help. New Yorkers have skated since colonial times, and Central Park's "skating pond" (now the lake) was once the most fashionable place to skate. Now that the holiday tourists have gone home, the lines are a little shorter at **Rockefeller Center** (especially on a weeknight) but if the lines are still too long, or the rink too small, try one of the parks department's seven rinks—including **Coney Island's** own, named for Brooklyn haberdasher Abe Stark—or one of the many that pop up in spots like **Brookfield Place** or **Bryant Park**. Skating makes a great date—for Valentine's or Galentine's or anything in between. Fashionistas can pose for frigid street-style photographs during Fashion Week, check out Hip Hop style at the Museum at FIT, and catch the John C. Weber collection of kimonos before it closes at the Metropolitan Museum of Art.

Professor Vaticinate says, *a Balmy Groundhog Day, but don't be deceived! You should always be wary of February. Indeed, by around Valentine's Day, it'll get cloudy, followed by a "Splashial" delivery: wild and rowdy with ill winds, turning wet and flaky every which way. Then a surge of warmth for the month's final week: 50s, 60s . . . might we even try for 70?*

Normals for Central Park
Avg. high: 42.2°
Avg. low: 29.5°
Avg. rainfall: 3.19"
Avg. snowfall: 10.1"

The 11th marks the 40th anniversary of what is known in weather annals as the Megalopolitan Snowstorm. One to two feet of snow fell from south-central Virginia to extreme southern New Hampshire. Thunderstorms were observed from Washington, DC, to NYC. LaGuardia Airport received 22 inches.

● **Sky Watch:** It will be most interesting to watch the gradual convergence of the two brightest planets, Venus and Jupiter, all of this month. On the 1st, they are evident in the west-southwest sky. If you hold your clenched fist out at arm's length, the two worlds are separated by three fists. But by the 28th, they'll be separated by the width of two full Moons. From the 21st to 23rd, a crescent Moon will glide past both planets—an eye-catching scene.

ANNALS OF THE NIGHT SKY

The largest object currently circling Earth is the International Space Station (ISS). It's also the brightest, sometimes shining as bright as Venus. For a specific schedule as to when it will be passing over your neighborhood, go to https://spotthestation.nasa.gov/.

NYC BOOK OF THE MONTH
Open City by Teju Cole (2011)

Cole's narrator, Julius, a young Nigerian completing a psychiatry fellowship at Columbia-Presbyterian Hospital, wanders through a city he considers, "a palimpsest . . . written, erased, rewritten." He visits Central Park in a blizzard when snow "erased the most obvious signs of the times, leaving one unable to guess which century it was." But what he finds as he walks is a city of immigrants, all pursuing their own visions of the American dream.

NYC MOVIE OF THE MONTH
Barefoot in the Park, directed by Gene Saks, starring Robert Redford and Jane Fonda (1967)

Neil Simon adapted his hit play about mismatched newlyweds—carefree Corrie and buttoned-up Paul—in their fifth-floor Greenwich Village apartment, where snow falls through a broken skylight. The climax, filmed on location, finds Paul "cutting loose" by drunkenly dancing barefoot around Washington Square Park in the freezing cold.

February has 28 days.

Jan. 30–Feb. 5

"That's one of the things about New York—you're so often confronted by a world that is completely alien to you, that you feel like you have no access to, but it's right next to you."
—Camille Rankine

30 MONDAY

☼ 7:08 AM / 5:08 PM

2015: Shake Shack begins trading on the New York Stock Exchange.

31 TUESDAY

☼ 7:07 AM / 5:12 PM

Last chance to see *Christine Sun Kim: Time Owes Me Rest Again* at the Queens Museum

1 WEDNESDAY

☼ 7:06 AM / 5:13 PM

City Center Encores! presents *The Light in the Piazza* directed by Chay Yew (through Feb. 5).

2 THURSDAY

☼ 7:05 AM / 5:14 PM ●

Groundhog Day

Yulianna Avdeeva, piano, plays Zankel Hall, Carnegie Hall.

3 FRIDAY

☼ 7:04 AM / 5:15 PM

Chamber Music Society of Lincoln Center presents Winter Festival: Schubert Forever.

4 SATURDAY

☼ 7:03 AM / 5:17 PM

SongStudio: Young Artists Recital at Zankel Hall, Carnegie Hall

5 SUNDAY

☼ 7:02 AM / 5:18 PM ○ FULL MOON

Last chance to see *Georg Baselitz: Drawings* at the Morgan Library and Museum

Feb. 6–12

"In Boston they ask, How much does he know? In New York, How much is he worth? In Philadelphia, Who were his parents?"
—Mark Twain

6 MONDAY
☼ 7:00 AM / 5:19 PM

1845: Isidor Straus, co-owner of Macy's and Abraham & Straus department stores with his brother Nathan, is born. (He will die in the sinking of the *Titanic* with his wife, Ida.)

7 TUESDAY
☼ 6:59 AM / 5:20 PM

Westminster Kennel Club Dog Show, Madison Square Garden (and 8th)

8 WEDNESDAY
☼ 6:55 AM / 5:22 PM

Fresh, Fly, and Fabulous: Fifty Years of Hip Hop Style opens at the Museum at FIT (through Apr. 23).

9 THURSDAY
☼ 6:57 AM / 5:23 PM

New York Fashion Week opens (through Feb. 15).

10 FRIDAY
☼ 6:56 AM / 5:24 PM

The New York Pops present *The Music of Star Wars* at Stern Auditorium/Perelman Stage at Carnegie Hall.

11 SATURDAY
☼ 6:55 AM / 5:25 PM

Jazz at Lincoln Center presents Dianne Reeves: Love is in the Air (and 10th).

12 SUNDAY
☼ 6:53 AM / 5:26 PM

Lincoln's Birthday

Langdon St. Ives: The Steampunk Musical! in Concert, by Josh Freilich and John Blaylock, at Feinstein's/54 Below

Feb. 13–19

"In a city of shadows and shadowy people, light between skyscrapers is enough of a treasure for me."
—Gay Talese

13 MONDAY

☼ 6:52 AM / 5:28 PM ☽ 3RD QUARTER

Chamber Music Society of Lincoln Center presents Master Class: Ken Noda.

14 TUESDAY

☼ 6:51 AM / 5:29 PM

Valentine's Day

The Queen's Six: From Windsor with Love at the Town Hall (and 15th)

15 WEDNESDAY

☼ 6:50 AM / 5:30 PM

Susan B. Anthony's Birthday

New York City Ballet presents *The Sleeping Beauty* (and Feb. 16–19; 21–26).

16 THURSDAY

☼ 6:48 AM / 5:31 PM ●

The Gregory Gift opens at the Frick Madison (through May 14).

17 FRIDAY

☼ 6:47 AM / 5:33 PM

Letters From Home: The 50 States Tour at Symphony Space

18 SATURDAY

☼ 6:46 AM / 5:34 PM ♓ PISCES

Adore Delano: Party Your World Tour at Gramercy Theater

19 SUNDAY

☼ 6:44 AM / 5:35 PM

Last chance to see *Xaviera Simmons: Crisis Makes a Book Club* at the Queens Museum

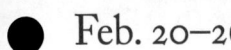

Feb. 20–26

"Every man there, in order to maintain the spirit of the place, should bear on his forehead a label stating how many dollars he is worth, and ... every label should be expected to assert a falsehood."
—Anthony Trollope, 1865

20 MONDAY
☼ 6:43 AM / 5:36 PM

Presidents' Day

NYC Public Schools' Midwinter Recess begins (through Feb. 24).

21 TUESDAY
☼ 6:42 AM / 5:37 PM ● NEW MOON

Carrie Underwood plays Madison Square Garden.

22 WEDNESDAY
☼ 6:40 AM / 5:38 PM

Ash Wednesday

Chamber Music Society of Lincoln Center presents *Inside Chamber Music: Brahms's Piano Trio in C Major*.

23 THURSDAY
☼ 6:39 AM / 5:40 PM

Chamber Music Society of Lincoln Center presents New Milestones: Memory.

24 FRIDAY
☼ 6:37 AM / 5:41 PM

Alan Doyle plays Sony Hall.

25 SATURDAY
☼ 6:36 AM / 5:42 PM

Last chance to see *New Practices New York* at the Center for Architecture

26 SUNDAY
☼ 6:34 AM / 5:43 PM

Metropolitan Opera presents a new *Lohengrin* by Wagner (through Apr. 1).

MARCH

As the professional basketball season winds down, New Yorkers keep their fingers crossed that at least *one* of their two teams make it to the playoffs. Brooklyn and Manhattan have been rivals—two iconic parks, two library systems, two totally different attitudes—since before they became one city in 1898 and have been antagonizing each other ever since; a win on the basketball court brings huge bragging rights. Fans of college ball, get ready: Madison Square Garden is hosting the **NCAA East Regional Tournament** for the first time since 2017. It's your last chance this year to see the paintings of Edward Hopper at the **Whitney Museum**. The **Museum of the City of New York** presents their first photography triennial, with work drawn from professional and amateur shutterbugs alike, and the **St. Patrick's Day Parade** on Fifth Avenue makes everyone Irish (for the day at least)

Professor Vaticinate says, *the March lion roars for much of the month; the Sun only puts in "cameo appearances." Around mid-month, watch the tides and beware of the Ides: rain/wet snow/gusty winds. It's a tempest tantrum! Spring arrives wet, then it remains unsettled through month's end. You could say that these are the hoarse and buggy days.*

Normals for
Central Park
Avg. high: 49.9°
Avg. low: 35.8°
Avg. rainfall: 4.29"
Avg. snowfall: 5.0"

March 12–13, 1993, saw one of the most paralyzing winter storms of the twentieth century. Known as Superstorm '93, it brought snow from southern Alabama to central Maine, with the heaviest amounts falling along the Appalachians where accumulations exceeded 40 inches. A combination of wet snow, sleet, and rain fell across the tristate area with over a foot of slush falling at LaGuardia.

Sky Watch: Like two ships passing in the evening twilight, Venus and Jupiter make their closest approach to each other on the evening of the 1st, side by side, a moon's-width apart. They'll call your attention in the west-southwest sky a half hour after sunset. Spring officially arrives in the Northern Hemisphere on the 20th, at 5:24 p.m. EDT.

ANNALS OF THE NIGHT SKY

Many cultures have calendars that are based on the movement of the Moon. For instance, Ramadan, the 9th month of the Muslim calendar and the holy month of fasting, begins with the first appearance of the Moon on the 22nd. A half hour after sunset, search low above the western horizon to catch a glimpse of this hairline crescent, only 29 hours past new phase.

NYC BOOK OF THE MONTH
Gentlemen Prefer Blondes by Anita Loos (1925)

The best-selling book of 1926, Loos's novel is a diary written by Lorelei Lee, a beautiful blond flapper with a knack for receiving expensive gifts from wealthy men. Starting on March 16, Lee's diary chronicles her adventures with various gentlemen and her sardonic best friend Dorothy—from New York's Ritz to Paris's "Foley Bergere."

NYC MOVIE OF THE MONTH
Saturday Night Fever, directed by John Badham, starring John Travolta (1977)

Based on a *New York* magazine article ("Tribal Rites of the New Saturday Night") by Nik Cohn—who later admitted to fabricating the story—Travolta's turn as Brooklyn paint store clerk with disco dreams started filming on location in Bay Ridge, Brooklyn, on March 14, 1977—and was nearly interrupted by Travolta fans eager to see the star of *Welcome Back, Kotter*.

March has 31 days.

Feb. 27–Mar. 5

"This is a vast city, more strange and original than handsome."
—Pyotr Tchaikovsky, 1891

---

27 MONDAY

☼ 6:33 AM / 5:44 PM   ◐ 1ST QUARTER

1860: Abraham Lincoln delivers the "Cooper Union Address," a major campaign speech.

---

28 TUESDAY

☼ 6:31 AM / 5:45 PM

Yo-Yo Ma performs Elgar's Cello Concerto at David Geffen Hall, Lincoln Center.

---

1 WEDNESDAY

☼ 6:30 AM / 5:47 PM

Black Orpheus opens at Circle in the Square Theatre.

---

2 THURSDAY

☼ 6:28 AM / 5:48 PM

Black Power to Black People: Branding the Black Panther Party opens at Poster House (through Sep. 10).

---

3 FRIDAY

☼ 6:27 AM / 5:49 PM

New York International Children's Film Festival begins (and Mar. 4, 5, 11, 12, 18, 19).

---

4 SATURDAY

☼ 6:25 AM / 5:50 PM

Last chance to see *Meret Oppenheim: My Exhibition* at the Museum of Modern Art

---

5 SUNDAY

☼ 6:24 AM / 5:51 PM

Last chance to see *Edward Hopper's New York* at the Whitney Museum

Mar. 6–12

"As we drew near New York I was ... staggered, by the cautious and grisly tales that went around. You must speak to no one in the streets, as they would not leave you till you were rooked and beaten."
—Robert Louis Stevenson

6 MONDAY
☼ 6:22 AM / 5:52 PM

1940: Ray Forrest of NBC makes the first U.S. airborne telecast while flying over NYC.

7 TUESDAY
☼ 6:20 AM / 5:53 PM ○ FULL MOON

Purim

Artist Spotlight: Hilary Hahn at David Geffen Hall, Lincoln Center

8 WEDNESDAY
☼ 6:19 AM / 5:54 PM

International Women's Day

Decoda: Transformations at Weill Recital Hall, Carnegie Hall

9 THURSDAY
☼ 6:17 AM / 5:56 PM

The Town Hall presents *Hits! The Musical*.

10 FRIDAY
☼ 6:16 AM / 5:57 PM

New York Now: Home—A Photography Triennial opens at the Museum of the City of New York.

11 SATURDAY
☼ 6:14 AM / 5:58 PM

Young People's Concert: The Art of Improvisation with Etienne Charles, David Geffen Hall, Lincoln Center

12 SUNDAY
☼ 7:12 AM / 6:59 PM

Daylight saving time begins.

Metropolitan Opera presents *Falstaff* (through Apr. 1).

Mar. 13–19

"Philadelphia has cheesesteaks—New York has irony."
—John F. Kennedy Jr.

13 MONDAY
☼ 7:11 AM / 7:00 PM

2020: Mayor Bill de Blasio declares State of Emergency in response to the COVID-19 pandemic.

14 TUESDAY
☼ 7:09 AM / 7:01 PM ◐ 3RD QUARTER

1921: Urbanist and architecture critic Ada Louise Huxtable is born in New York.

15 WEDNESDAY
☼ 7:08 AM / 7:02 PM

City Center Encores! presents *Dear World* (through Mar. 19).

16 THURSDAY
☼ 7:06 AM / 7:03 PM

American Composers Orchestra performs *Modern Yesterdays*, Zankel Hall, Carnegie Hall.

17 FRIDAY
☼ 7:04 AM / 7:04 PM

Saint Patrick's Day

Saint Patrick's Day Parade, 5th Ave.

18 SATURDAY
☼ 7:03 AM / 7:05 PM

Steve Barakatt: Piano Néoréalité World Tour at Zankel Hall, Carnegie Hall

19 SUNDAY
☼ 7:01 AM / 7:06 PM

Static-X: Rise of the Machine at Irving Plaza

Mar. 20–26

"The city also puts a lot of effort into making your hometown look really drab and tiny, just in case you were wondering why it's such a drag to go back sometimes."
—Colson Whitehead

20 MONDAY
☼ 6:59 AM / 7:07 PM ♈ ARIES

Vernal Equinox

Ensemble MidtVest plays Weill Recital Hall, Carnegie Hall.

21 TUESDAY
☼ 6:58 AM / 7:08 PM ● NEW MOON

New York Sounds of Spring Festival, Stern Auditorium/Perelman Stage, Carnegie Hall

22 WEDNESDAY
☼ 6:56 AM / 7:10 PM

Ramadan begins.

2001: Fresh Kills Landfill—the largest man-made structure on earth—closes.

23 THURSDAY
☼ 6:54 AM / 7:11 PM

Madison Square Garden hosts the NCAA East Regional Tournament (through Mar. 25).

24 FRIDAY
☼ 6:53 AM / 7:12 PM

JVNA plays Webster Hall.

25 SATURDAY
☼ 6:51 AM / 7:13 PM

City Center presents Flamenco Festival with Sara Baras and her company performing *Alma* (Mar. 23–26).

26 SUNDAY
☼ 6:49 AM / 7:14 PM

Alexandre Tharaud, piano, plays Zankel Hall, Carnegie Hall.

Mar. 27–Apr. 2

"Turn which way you will, mechanics, carvers, carpenters, bricklayers, ship carpenters, cartmen, all is one continual bustle, from morning till ten o'clock at night. No wonder New York outstrips all her rivals." —Anne Royall, 1824

---

27 MONDAY

☼ 6:48 AM / 7:15 PM

Metropolitan Opera presents Strauss's *Der Rosenkavalier* (through Apr. 20).

---

28 TUESDAY

☼ 6:46 AM / 7:16 PM ☽ 1ST QUARTER

Concerto Köln performs *Mirrors* at Zankel Hall, Carnegie Hall.

---

29 WEDNESDAY

☼ 6:44 AM / 7:17 PM

Standard Time with Michael Feinstein, Zankel Hall, Carnegie Hall

---

30 THURSDAY

☼ 6:43 AM / 7:18 PM ●

City Center presents the National Ballet of Canada with live music by the National Ballet of Canada Orchestra (through Apr. 1).

---

31 FRIDAY

☼ 6:41 AM / 7:19 PM

Last chance to see *Botanical Lessons* at the Cooper Hewitt

---

1 SATURDAY

☼ 6:39 AM / 7:20 PM

April Fool's Day

Barnyard Egg Hunt at Queens County Farm (and 8th)

---

2 SUNDAY

☼ 6:38 AM / 7:21 PM

Palm Sunday

Last chance to see *Lives of the Gods: Divinity in Maya Art* and *Water Memories* at the Metropolitan Museum of Art

APRIL

Baseball's Opening Day fills some hearts with anticipation of postseason glory. Mets and Yankees fans ditch work early to ride the 4-5-6 to the Bronx or the 7 into Queens to sit in the stands in suits and pencil skirts—or they just come for the food. Tastes have evolved since the glory days of hot dogs, Schaefer beer, and peanuts at Ebbets Field. Today the city's ballparks are filled to the brim with craft beer, artisanal donuts, and even vegan nachos. It's also **Poetry Month**—library branches throughout the city offer readings and workshops, while WNYC broadcasts New Yorkers' best efforts at verse daily. Combine the two by stashing a copy of "Baseball and Writing" by Brooklyn's own Marianne Moore on **Poem in Your Pocket Day**. Wear your best bonnet to Fifth Avenue's **Easter Parade**, and get your hands dirty composting, planting, or weeding on **Earth Day** at Queens County Farm or Staten Island's landfill-turned-soon-to-be-park Freshkills, and don't forget to keep an eye on the **Brooklyn Botanic Garden's Cherrywatch** website to time your visit for peak blossoms (and Instagram stories).

Professor Vaticinate says, *no foolin'! A round of tempestuous weather kicks off this month. Finally! Some fine and pleasant weather arrives just in time for Easter, and it sticks around through the third week of April. Then, as the month winds down, the skies are scoured by showers.*

Normals for
Central Park
Avg. high: 61.8°
Avg. low: 45.5°
Avg. rainfall: 4.1"
Avg. snowfall: 0.4"

April 25, 1875, saw NYC's latest measurable snowfall (more than a trace), when 3" fell. The *New York Times* called it "A Touch of Winter in the Heart of Spring." It was also the snowiest April on record with 13.5".

Sky Watch: The first Full Moon of Spring is on Thursday, the 6th—the so-called Paschal Moon. Ecclesiastical rules mandate that the first Sunday after this Moon is Easter, and so it will be on the 9th. In the predawn hours of the 10th, the bright reddish star to the Moon's lower right is the "Rival of Mars," Antares. Mars itself forms a long isosceles triangle with the "Twin stars," Pollux and Castor, in the western evening sky of the 23rd. A crescent Moon will pass through the triangle during the evenings of the 25th and 26th.

ANNALS OF THE NIGHT SKY

One of the most spectacular meteor showers ever seen occurred on April 20, 1803, when the townspeople of Richmond, Virginia, were roused from bed by a fire alarm and were able to observe this spectacular display between 1 and 3 a.m. According to witnesses, meteors "seemed to fall from every point in the heavens, in such numbers as to resemble a shower of sky rockets."

NYC BOOK OF THE MONTH
Manhattan Transfer by Jon Dos Passos (1925)

Dos Passos's modernist novel tries to capture the whole of the city from the Gilded Age to the Jazz Age through fragmented, overlapping narratives. Each chapter opens with a poetic, cinematic collage of words and images evoking a restless, merciless city. Dos Passos created a way of looking at the city that is reflected by later authors like Don DeLillo.

NYC MOVIE OF THE MONTH
Easter Parade, directed by Charles Walters, starring Judy Garland, Fred Astaire, and Ann Miller (1948)

Easter Parade is a backstage musical set in NYC's vaudeville era—more than half of the songs were written by New Yorker Irving Berlin decades earlier. Although the movie was filmed on Hollywood sets, its finale finds Garland, in an enormous white hat, parading arm in arm with Astaire in the Easter Parade on Fifth Avenue.

April has 30 days.

Apr. 3–9

"Post-thaw, olfactory New York springs to life.... At certain subway stops, the odor of rotting flesh returns.... All over town you can enjoy the blossoming of that chief attribute of New York: the smell of urine." —Nick Paumgarten

3 MONDAY
☼ 6:36 AM / 7:22 PM

Chamber Music Society of Lincoln Center presents Master Class: Kalichstein-Laredo-Robinson Trio.

4 TUESDAY
☼ 6:35 AM / 7:23 PM

Melissa Aldana plays the Village Vanguard.

5 WEDNESDAY
☼ 6:33 AM / 7:24 PM

Passover begins.

1911: More than 400,000 people march in a labor union parade to mourn victims of the Triangle Shirtwaist Factory Fire.

6 THURSDAY
☼ 6:31 AM / 7:25 PM ○ FULL MOON

Chamber Music Society of Lincoln Center presents New Milestones: Evocation.

7 FRIDAY
☼ 6:30 AM / 7:26 PM

Good Friday

New York International Auto Show at the Javits Center (through Apr. 16)

8 SATURDAY
☼ 6:28 AM / 7:27 PM

Vesak

1991: NYC's last automat, at 200 East 42nd Street, closes.

9 SUNDAY
☼ 6:27 AM / 7:28 PM

Easter Sunday

Easter Parade and Easter Bonnet Festival on 5th Ave. from 49th to 57th Sts.

Apr. 10–16

"I miss the animal buoyancy of New York, the animal vitality. I did not mind that it had no meaning and no depth."
—Anaïs Nin

10 MONDAY

☼ 6:25 AM / 7:29 PM

NYC Public Schools' Spring Break begins (through Apr. 17).

11 TUESDAY

☼ 6:23 AM / 7:31 PM

Artist Spotlight: Sir András Schiff at David Geffen Hall, Lincoln Center (through Apr. 18)

12 WEDNESDAY

☼ 6:22 AM / 7:32 PM

Seong-Jin Cho, piano, plays Stern Auditorium/Perelman Stage, Carnegie Hall.

13 THURSDAY

☼ 6:20 AM / 7:33 PM
☽ 3RD QUARTER

Passover ends.

City Center presents Artists at the Center with tap dancer Ayodele Casel (through Apr. 15).

14 FRIDAY

☼ 6:19 AM / 7:34 PM

Chamber Orchestra of New York performs Journeys: 15th Anniversary Concert at Zankel Hall, Carnegie Hall.

15 SATURDAY

☼ 6:17 AM / 7:35 PM *Tax Day*

Mets and Yankees wear number 42 for Jackie Robinson day.

New York City Tartan Day Parade (25th anniversary)

16 SUNDAY

☼ 6:16 AM / 7:36 PM

Orthodox Easter Sunday

Last chance to see *Jimmy DeSana: Submission* at the Brooklyn Museum

Apr. 17–23

"Every un-renovated tenement is an offense to someone's sense of progress, each new building a desecration of someone's childhood."
—Justin Davidson

17 MONDAY
☼ 6:14 AM / 7:37 PM

Radio City Music Hall presents Dead Can Dance: Life & Works North America.

18 TUESDAY
☼ 6:13 AM / 7:38 PM

Lailat al-Qadr

New York City Ballet presents *Masters at Work: Balanchine & Robbins I* (and Apr. 19, 20, 22, 26; May 5).

19 WEDNESDAY
☼ 6:11 AM / 7:39 PM

Total solar eclipse begins at 9:34 PM.

City Center presents Dance Theatre of Harlem (through Apr. 23).

20 THURSDAY
☼ 6:10 AM / 7:40 PM ● NEW MOON
♉ TAURUS

Total solar eclipse ends at 2:59 AM.

Nils Frahm plays Kings Theatre, Brooklyn.

21 FRIDAY
☼ 6:08 AM / 7:41 PM

Ramadan ends.

Metropolitan Opera presents *La Bohème* (through Jun. 9).

22 SATURDAY
☼ 6:07 AM / 7:42 PM

Earth Day

Eid al-Fitr

Celebrate Earth Day with a day of service at Queens County Farm.

23 SUNDAY
☼ 6:05 AM / 7:43 PM

Last chance to see *Death to the Living, Long Live Trash* at the Brooklyn Museum

Apr. 24–30

"Every time one looks at the harbor and the New York skyline across the river it is quite different and the range of atmospheric effects is endless."
 —Hart Crane, 1924

24 MONDAY
☼ 6:04 AM / 7:44 PM

Boston Symphony Orchestra plays Stern Auditorium/Perelman Stage, Carnegie Hall.

25 TUESDAY
☼ 6:03 AM / 7:45 PM

New York Philharmonic Spring Gala, Lincoln Center.

26 WEDNESDAY
☼ 6:01 AM / 7:46 PM

Les Arts Florissants perform Music for the Holy Week at Zankel Hall, Carnegie Hall.

27 THURSDAY
☼ 6:00 AM / 7:47 PM
☽ 1ST QUARTER

Poem in Your Pocket Day: carry a poem by an NYC bard like Edna St. Vincent Millay, Walt Whitman, Langston Hughes, or Frank O'Hara.

28 FRIDAY
☼ 5:58 AM / 7:48 PM

Verona Quartet play *Inside Out*, Weill Recital Hall, Carnegie Hall.

29 SATURDAY
☼ 5:57 AM / 7:49 PM

Arbor Day

Brooklyn Botanic Garden Cherry Blossom Weekends (and Apr. 30th; May 6–7)

30 SUNDAY
☼ 5:56 AM / 7:50 PM

Last chance to see *Swagger and Tenderness: The South Bronx Portraits by John Ahearn and Rigoberto Torres* at the Bronx Museum of the Arts

MAY

THE WARM MAY SUN draws New Yorkers outdoors. It's a great time of year to toss your kids on the back of an electric cargo bike or hop on a Citi Bike to try your luck on the delivery truck–clogged streets. Or wait for the **Five Boro Bike Tour's** forty miles of blissfully traffic-free thoroughfares. Grab the binoculars to observe migratory songbirds pausing in Central Park or wildly dressed celebrities peacocking on the Met's steps for the **Costume Institute's gala**. Celebrate **Cinco de Mayo** in Brooklyn's Sunset Park (and grab a Vietnamese bahn mi at Ba Xuyen while you're there). To kick off the summer on Memorial Day, get to Brooklyn Bridge Park (extremely) early to snag a grill, or honor those who have served at **Bay Ridge's Memorial Day Parade**, one of the country's oldest parades. Then cap off **Fleet Week** with the Intrepid Museum's annual Memorial Day ceremony.

PROFESSOR VATICINATE SAYS, *the first 10 days of May are forecast to be showery and even squally. For the rest of the month, the weather can't decide between Sun and storm. The best weather (we think) falls during the 20th–23rd, followed by yet more wet weather—hopefully—moving out in time for the Memorial Day holiday weekend.*

NORMALS FOR CENTRAL PARK
Avg. high: 71.4°
Avg. low: 55.0°
Avg. rainfall: 3.96"

The Atlantic hurricane season begins on June 1, but it might not be that way for much longer. Since 2011, a total of 10 named storms have formed in the Atlantic prior to the hurricane season start date. Eight of those 10 happened since 2015, with 2015–2020 all featuring a pre-June named tropical system. As a consequence, some have been lobbying to shift the start date to the 15th of May.

Sky Watch: A changing sky show will play out in our western evening sky about 45 minutes after sundown from the 21st to 24th. On the 21st, look for brilliant Venus shining below the "Twin stars," Pollux and Castor. To the upper left of the Twins shines Mars and far to the lower right of Venus will be a skinny crescent Moon. On the 22nd, the Moon will have shifted closer to Venus and by the 23rd, will have moved to its upper left and just below Pollux. And finally, on the 24th, the widening Moon sits directly above Mars.

ANNALS OF THE NIGHT SKY

Forty years ago, on May 11, 1983, our Earth had a very close brush with a small comet bearing the name of IRAS-Araki-Alcock. It passed to within 2.9 million miles of the Earth—closer than any other comet except for one back in 1770—and ever-so-briefly it became brighter than Polaris the North Star.

NYC BOOK OF THE MONTH
Another Country by James Baldwin (1962)

Baldwin's novel runs along the A train—from Harlem to Greenwich Village and back again. "Everybody's on the A train—you take it uptown, I take it downtown" says Rufus Scott, a jazz musician around whose suicide the rest of the book takes shape. The book explores racism, bisexuality, and infidelity in the midcentury bohemian city.

NYC MOVIE OF THE MONTH
On the Town, directed by Gene Kelly and Stanley Donen, starring Gene Kelly and Frank Sinatra (1949)

Three sailors on 24-hour shore leave in New York City pursue Ms. Turnstiles (based on the real-life Ms. Subways beauty contest). Adapted from the Broadway musical by Leonard Bernstein, Betty Comden, and Adolph Green, it was the first Hollywood musical filmed on location in NYC—but only 7 minutes of city footage made it onscreen.

May has 31 days.

May 1–7

"We could go on and on. We could talk about the arts and the money and the sheer imaginative power that is unleashed daily in this town.... This must, this really must, be the place."

—*New York* magazine, 1977

---

1 MONDAY
☼ 5:54 AM / 7:51 PM

Metropolitan Museum of Art's Costume Institute Gala

---

2 TUESDAY
☼ 5:53 AM / 7:53 PM

New York City Ballet presents *21st Century Choreography I* (and May 11, 13, 17, 18).

---

3 WEDNESDAY
☼ 5:52 AM / 7:54 PM

City Center Encores! presents *Oliver!* (through May 14).

---

4 THURSDAY
☼ 5:51 AM / 7:55 PM

Celebrate urbanist Jane Jacob's birthday with the Municipal Arts Society by going on a Jane's Walk.

---

5 FRIDAY
☼ 5:50 AM / 7:56 PM   ○ FULL MOON

Cinco de Mayo

Metropolitan Opera presents a new *Don Giovanni* directed by Ivo van Hove (through Jun. 2).

---

6 SATURDAY
☼ 5:48 AM / 7:57 PM

Jazz at Lincoln Center presents Tito Puente and Tito Rodriguez Centennial Celebration featuring Carlos Henriquez (and 5th).

---

7 SUNDAY
☼ 5:47 AM / 7:58 PM

The Five Boro Bike Tour

May 8–14

"The whole world revolves around New York. Very little happens anywhere unless someone in New York presses the button."
—Duke Ellington

8 MONDAY

☼ 5:46 AM / 7:59 PM

Joshua Bell plays David Geffen Hall at Lincoln Center (and 7th).

9 TUESDAY

☼ 5:45 AM / 8:00 PM

VV/Neon Noir Tour plays Irving Plaza (and 8th).

10 WEDNESDAY

☼ 5:44 AM / 8:01 PM

New York City Ballet presents *Masters at Work Balanchine & Robbins III* (and May 23, 27).

11 THURSDAY

☼ 5:43 AM / 8:02 PM

Khatia Buniatishvili, piano, plays Stern Auditorium/Perelman Stage, Carnegie Hall.

12 FRIDAY

☼ 5:42 AM / 8:03 PM   ☽ 3RD QUARTER

New York City Ballet presents *New Peck* (and May 14, 20, 24, 25).

13 SATURDAY

☼ 5:41 AM / 8:04 PM

1985: *New York* magazine declares that the "Yupper West Side" has been overrun by young professionals.

14 SUNDAY

☼ 5:40 AM / 8:05 PM

Mother's Day

American Protégé Winners Recital at Weill Hall, Carnegie Hall

May 15–21

"Here we are in New York. From a Frenchman's perspective, it looks disarmingly weird. There isn't a dome, a steeple or a large edifice in sight."
—Alexis de Tocqueville, 1831

15 MONDAY
☼ 5:39 AM / 8:06 PM

1904: Coney Island's Dreamland opens.

16 TUESDAY
☼ 5:38 AM / 8:07 PM

1946: Irving Berlin's *Annie Get Your Gun* opens at the Imperial Theatre.

17 WEDNESDAY
☼ 5:37 AM / 8:08 PM

1884: P. T. Barnum leads 21 elephants over the Brooklyn Bridge to prove it won't fall down.

18 THURSDAY
☼ 5:36 AM / 8:09 PM

Ascension Day

Signum Quartet plays Weill Recital Hall, Carnegie Hall.

19 FRIDAY
☼ 5:35 AM / 8:09 PM   ● NEW MOON

Metropolitan Opera presents a new *Zauberflöte* by Mozart (through Jun. 10).

20 SATURDAY
☼ 5:34 AM / 8:10 PM

Dance Parade New York

21 SUNDAY
☼ 5:34 AM / 8:11 PM   ♊ GEMINI

Kings Theatre, Brooklyn, presents *Madagascar: The Musical*.

May 22–28

"Commuters give the city its tidal restlessness; natives give it solidity and continuity; but the settlers give it passion."
—E. B. White

---

22 MONDAY

☼ 5:33 AM / 8:12 PM

City Center Studio 5 presents a talk about From the Street: City Center Dance Festival, moderated by Ephrat Asherie and Adesola Osakalumi.

---

23 TUESDAY

☼ 5:32 AM / 8:13 PM

1922: *Abie's Irish Rose*, a comedy about an interfaith marriage, debuts on Broadway. It will run for 5 years.

---

24 WEDNESDAY

☼ 5:31 AM / 8:14 PM

Fleet Week begins (through May 30).

---

25 THURSDAY

☼ 5:31 AM / 8:15 PM

Shavuot begins.

Joseph Alessi plays Chick Corea, David Geffen Hall, Lincoln Center (through May 27).

---

26 FRIDAY

☼ 5:30 AM / 8:16 PM

1969: *Midnight Cowboy*, starring John Voight and Dustin Hoffman, premieres in New York with an X rating.

---

27 SATURDAY

☼ 5:29 AM / 8:17 PM ◐ 1ST QUARTER

Shavuot ends.

1989: Keith Haring paints the mural *Once Upon a Time* on the bathroom walls at the Lesbian and Gay Community Services Center at 208 West 13th Street.

---

28 SUNDAY

☼ 5:29 AM / 8:17 PM

1962: Eero Saarinen's TWA terminal at JFK is dedicated.

JUNE

For New Yorkers lucky enough to enjoy Summer Fridays or flexible work-from-home schedules, Friday afternoons in June are perfect for lounging outside at happy hour at a rickety café table or subtly enjoying a to-go drink in Tompkins Square Park or Washington Square. For sophisticates, the **Met's Roof Garden** is a perfect place to mingle with avant-garde art and good-looking art lovers—just don't get caught in a surprise summer thunderstorm and find yourself in a stairwell clutching a full art-themed cocktail. June is also a great month for celebrations. Celebrate **Juneteenth** in East New York and Brownsville. Museum hop during the Upper East Side's best block party, the **Museum Mile Festival**; toss long strands of fake pearls over your bathing suit and dance your tail off at **Coney Island's Mermaid Parade and Ball**; and mix politics, fun, and fashion at the **New York City Pride March** through Greenwich Village.

Professor Vaticinate says, *the month starts off with a risk of thunderstorms, no doubt an "enlightning" experience. The wetness continues through the 7th, which only proves that June doesn't always bust out—sometimes it leaks in. The weather dries out in time for the Belmont Stakes, but summer's arrival on the 21st is a wet one, followed by a torrid spell: first a water torture, then a scorcher.*

Normals for Central Park Avg. high: 79.7° Avg. low: 64.4° Avg. rainfall: 4.54"	The summer of 1993 was one of only two cases in the 154-year history of NYC-weather records, where the number of days that the temperature hit or exceeded 90° reached 39. The only other summer with as many hot days was in 1991. On average, there are 17 such days during a typical summer.

Sky Watch: Summer officially arrives on the 21st at 10:57 a.m. The length of daylight now lasts longest: 15 hours and 6 minutes. After today, the days will be getting shorter; they will not begin to lengthen again until three days before Christmas. Right after sunset on the 21st, look toward the west-northwest for a lovely crescent Moon accompanied to its lower left by dazzling Venus. This beautiful celestial tableau will remain in view until they set just after 11 p.m.

ANNALS OF THE NIGHT SKY

The largest known star in the universe, UY Scuti, is a hypergiant with a radius around 1,700 times larger than the radius of the Sun. To put that in perspective, if our Sun were the size of a baseball, UY Scuti would be a globe 390 feet in diameter!

NYC BOOK OF THE MONTH
The Great Gatsby by F. Scott Fitzgerald (1925)

A job trading bonds in New York City brings Nick Carraway to a Long Island bungalow in the spring of 1922 and into the lives of his flashy neighbor Jay Gatsby and unhappy cousin Daisy Buchanan. Fitzgerald's jazz-age city is full of parties, speakeasies, speeding motorcars, and devastating secrets.

NYC MOVIE OF THE MONTH
West Side Story, directed by Robert Wise and Jerome Robbins, starring Natalie Wood, Richard Beymer, and Rita Moreno (1961)

Based on Leonard Bernstein's hit musical, *West Side Story* sets the story of Romeo and Juliet amid rival gangs in San Juan Hill—a West Side Manhattan neighborhood soon to be bulldozed for Lincoln Center. The prologue with Jets and Sharks dancing through city streets was filmed on West 68th Street and a playground on East 110th Street—but the rest of the film was shot on a Hollywood soundstage.

June has 30 days.

May 29–Jun. 4

"The Statue of Liberty is a washout—she gets her stays at the same place as Queen Mary."
—Rebecca West, 1923

29 MONDAY
☼ 5:28 AM / 8:18 PM

Memorial Day

Blue Note Jazz Festival begins (through June).

30 TUESDAY
☼ 5:28 AM / 8:19 PM

Metropolitan Opera presents Wagner's *Fliegende Holländer* (through Jun. 10).

31 WEDNESDAY
☼ 5:27 AM / 8:20 PM

Renee Fleming, soprano, and Evgeny Kissin, piano, play Stern Auditorium/Perelman Stage, Carnegie Hall.

1 THURSDAY
☼ 5:27 AM / 8:20 PM

City Center presents Ballet Hispánico (through Jun. 3).

2 FRIDAY
☼ 5:26 AM / 8:22 PM

Jazz at Lincoln Center presents The Jazz Ambassadors: Duke, Dizzy, and Brubeck with Wynton Marsalis (and Jun. 1, 3).

3 SATURDAY
☼ 5:26 AM / 8:22 PM ○ FULL MOON

Lullaby Project Celebration Concert, Zankel Hall, Carnegie Hall

4 SUNDAY
☼ 5:26 AM / 8:23 PM

Last chance to see *Gateway to Himalayan Art* at the Rubin Museum

Jun. 5–11

"What does it mean to be found obscene in New York? If anyone is the first person to be found obscene in New York, he must feel utterly depraved."
—Lenny Bruce

5 MONDAY
☼ 5:25 AM / 8:23 PM

1856: The parks department's oldest statue—of George Washington—is installed at the southeast corner of Union Square.

6 TUESDAY
☼ 5:25 AM / 8:24 PM

D-Day

2000: Jeff Koon's *Puppy* is installed at Rockefeller Plaza.

7 WEDNESDAY
☼ 5:25 AM / 8:24 PM

1985: The Beastie Boys open for Madonna at Radio City Music Hall.

8 THURSDAY
☼ 5:24 AM / 8:25 PM

From Water to Desert, David Geffen Hall, Lincoln Center (through Jun. 10)

9 FRIDAY
☼ 5:24 AM / 8:26 PM

Lindeblad School of Music Showcase Concert, Weill Hall, Carnegie Hall

10 SATURDAY
☼ 5:24 AM / 8:26 PM ◐ 3RD QUARTER

The Belmont Stakes horse race

11 SUNDAY
☼ 5:24 AM / 8:27 PM

National Puerto Rican Day Parade on 5th Ave.

Jun. 12–18

"I struck New York with the record, and New York struck me with a tidal wave and I threw this big dust storm into New York's face, just to show this little snotnose town who is who around here." —Woody Guthrie

---

12 MONDAY
☼ 5:24 AM / 8:27 PM

1940: New York City purchases the private subway operators IRT and BMT, forming the modern transit system.

---

13 TUESDAY
☼ 5:24 AM / 8:28 PM

Museum Mile Festival

---

14 WEDNESDAY
☼ 5:24 AM / 8:28 PM

1973: Bruce Springsteen plays his first concert at Madison Square Garden.

---

15 THURSDAY
☼ 5:24 AM / 8:28 PM

The MET Orchestra plays Stern Auditorium/Perelman Stage, Carnegie Hall.

---

16 FRIDAY
☼ 5:24 AM / 8:29 PM

Symphony Space presents Bloomsday on Broadway.

---

17 SATURDAY
☼ 5:24 AM / 8:29 PM

Coney Island Mermaid Parade and Ball

---

18 SUNDAY
☼ 5:24 AM / 8:29 PM   ● NEW MOON

Father's Day

Harlem Skyscraper Classic Bicycle Race around Marcus Garvey Park

Jun. 19–25

"Any garden is a triumph of man's will over nature's forces, but an urban, rooftop patch of greenery is a monument to a gardener's sheer cussedness."
—Marilyn Bethany

---

19 MONDAY
☼ 5:24 AM / 8:30 PM

Juneteenth

Juneteenth NY Festival (Jun. 16–19)

---

20 TUESDAY
☼ 5:24 AM / 8:30 PM

1964: The Rolling Stones play the last gig of their first U.S. tour at Carnegie Hall.

---

21 WEDNESDAY
☼ 5:25 AM / 8:30 PM ♋ CANCER

Summer Solstice

Practice yoga at the Solstice in Times Square.

---

22 THURSDAY
☼ 5:25 AM / 8:30 PM

1665: Thomas Willett is appointed the first (English) mayor of New York.

---

23 FRIDAY
☼ 5:25 AM / 8:31 PM

1978: The *Daily News* runs the headline "Berkowitz Goes Wild in Court: 'I'll Kill Them All' He Shouts."

---

24 SATURDAY
☼ 5:25 AM / 8:31 PM

1934: Amelia Earhart kicks off the second annual Annette Gipson Trophy Race for women aviators at Floyd Bennet Field.

---

25 SUNDAY
☼ 5:26 AM / 8:31 PM

NYC Pride March

Jun. 26–Jul. 2

"New York has a thousand universes in it that don't always connect but we do all walk the same streets, hear the same sirens, ride the same subways, see the same headlines in the *Post*...."
—Jay-Z

26 MONDAY
☼ 5:26 AM / 8:31 PM   ☽ 1ST QUARTER

1978: Location filming for *The Warriors* starts on city streets.

27 TUESDAY
☼ 5:26 AM / 8:31 PM

The Eels play Webster Hall (and 28th).

28 WEDNESDAY
☼ 5:26 AM / 8:31 PM

1984: The one and only episode of Michael Holman's *Graffiti Rock* one airs on WPIX, channel 11.

29 THURSDAY
☼ 5:27 AM / 8:31 PM

Eid al-Adha

1969: Harlem Cultural Festival begins.

30 FRIDAY
☼ 5:28 AM / 8:31 PM

1988: The *New York Times* announces Anna Wintour will head *Vogue* magazine.

1 SATURDAY
☼ 5:28 AM / 8:31 PM

1941: The world's first TV commercial—for Bulova watches—is broadcast during a Dodgers–Phillies game at Ebbets Field.

2 SUNDAY
☼ 5:29 AM / 8:30 PM

1971: Bed-Stuy's Kosciuszko Pool, designed by Bed-Stuy native and Miami Beach architect Morris Lapidus, opens.

JULY

As the garbage ripens on the sidewalks and street puddles ferment into syrupy gray goo, New Yorkers start to wonder why they're still here. Luckily the **outdoor summer movie season** is in full swing. Flicks can be found overlooking the East River in Brooklyn Bridge Park, deep in Midtown's Bryant Park—be prepared for the five o'clock stampede to claim a patch of grass—and presented by Rooftop Films in unique venues, like Green-Wood Cemetery. The cool, breezy atmosphere of the city's rooftops can feel far away from the stifling sidewalks—whether you are watching a movie, sipping cocktails at the rooftop bar of a fancy hotel, or sunbathing on a humble tenement building's "tar beach." Find a rooftop with a view for **Independence Day fireworks**, relive the nineties with **Matchbox Twenty** at Jones Beach Theater, and don't forget to point your cameras down a side street to the west at sunset for **Manhattanhenge**.

PROFESSOR VATICINATE SAYS, *at the start, it's more likely hot than not; keep a beach within reach. Ms. Nature might provide pyrotechnics displays of her own on the 4th (lightning and thunder), followed by a brief break in the heat. It's back by the second week of July, though: sultry and sticky. Hold your breath while we're under a cone of ozone. For the month's final week, watch for gully washers.*

NORMALS FOR CENTRAL PARK	
Avg. high: 84.9° Avg. low: 70.1° Avg. rainfall: 4.60"	On July 21, 1983, famed songstress Diana Ross took the stage in Central Park before an audience of over 800,000. Soon after the entertainer began, severe thunderstorms threatened to put an end to the show, but Ross pushed on for much of the set, urging the soaked crowd to remain calm and stay for the concert.

SKY WATCH: Venus, shining in the western sky after sunset like a sequined showgirl, reaches the pinnacle of her great brilliance on the 7th, then rapidly drops lower in the sky during the next two-and-a-half weeks, completely disappearing from view by the 25th. Venus won't be far from much dimmer Mars on the 9th, when the red planet engages in a tight conjunction with the bluish star Regulus, making for an eye-catching color contrast.

ANNALS OF THE NIGHT SKY

In 1975, when U.S. astronauts went to Russia to train for the Apollo-Soyuz test project, they presumed their rooms were bugged. One astronaut complained to the walls that there weren't enough coat hangers; when he returned from dinner, the room was strewn with them. He gratefully thanked the lampshade.

NYC BOOK OF THE MONTH
The Fortress of Solitude by Jonathan Lethem (2003)

Lethem's semi-autobiographical novel about two comic book–loving friends from different backgrounds who accidentally acquire a super-power opens with an image of gentrification, one of the book's themes: "two white girls in flannel nightgowns and red vinyl roller skates with white laces, tracing tentative circles on a cracked blue slate sidewalk at seven o'clock on an evening in July" in Gowanus, Brooklyn.

NYC MOVIE OF THE MONTH
Do the Right Thing, directed by Spike Lee,
starring Lee, John Turturro, Ruby Dee, Ossie Davis,
Rosie Perez, and Danny Aiello (1989)

Set on the hottest day of the year in Brooklyn's Bedford Stuyvesant, Spike Lee's masterpiece of racial tensions boiling over was inspired by several real-life instances of racial violence in Ed Koch's NYC. Lee insisted on filming on a stretch of Stuyvesant Ave. between Lexington Ave. and Quincy St. in Bed-Stuy—constructing Sal's Famous Pizzeria and a Korean grocery store on vacant lots onsite.

July has 31 days.

Jul. 3–9

"The Dawn! My spirit to its spirit thrills. Almost the mighty city is asleep, no pushing crowd, no tramping feet. But here and there a few cars groaning creep along, above, and underneath the street."
—Claude McKay

---

3 MONDAY

☼ 5:29 AM / 8:30 PM ○ FULL MOON

1952: Andy Warhol's first solo exhibition, *Fifteen Drawings Based on the Writings of Truman Capote*, closes at the Hugo Gallery.

---

4 TUESDAY

☼ 5:30 AM / 8:30 PM

Independence Day

Nathan's Hot Dog Eating Contest at the corner of Surf and Stillwell Aves. in Coney Island

---

5 WEDNESDAY

☼ 5:30 AM / 8:30 PM

1857: The Dead Rabbits riot—the city's largest outbreak of gang violence until the draft riots of 1863—ends a day after it begins.

---

6 THURSDAY

☼ 5:31 AM / 8:30 PM

1855: The *New York Daily Tribune* advertises the first edition of Walt Whitman's *Leaves of Grass*.

---

7 FRIDAY

☼ 5:31 AM / 8:29 PM

Rossitza Banova, piano, plays Weill Hall, Carnegie Hall.

---

8 SATURDAY

☼ 5:32 AM / 8:29 PM

1889: The first number of the *Wall Street Journal* is published.

---

9 SUNDAY

☼ 5:33 AM / 8:29 PM ◐ 3RD QUARTER

1776: Patriots tear down the statue of King George III in Bowling Green and melt (most) of it down for bullets. (Parts of it are still at the New-York Historical Society.)

Jul. 10–16

"New York City ... like a great witch ... enticing thousands ... Some she at once crushes beneath her feet ... a few she favors and fondles, riding them high on the bubbles of fortune."
—James Weldon Johnson

10 MONDAY
☼ 5:33 AM / 8:28 PM

1981: *Escape from New York* premieres in the U.S.

11 TUESDAY
☼ 5:34 AM / 8:28 PM

1936: Triborough Bridge opens.

12 WEDNESDAY
☼ 5:35 AM / 8:27 PM

1855: Ralph Waldo Emerson tells Walt Whitman, "I greet you at the beginning of a great career."

13 THURSDAY
☼ 5:36 AM / 8:27 PM

See a Manhattanhenge sunset at 14th, 23rd, 34th, 42nd, or 57th Street.

14 FRIDAY
☼ 5:36 AM / 8:26 PM

1853: The Exhibition of the Industry of All Nations opens in the Crystal Palace (at today's Bryant Park).

15 SATURDAY
☼ 5:37 AM / 8:26 PM

1922: An Australian duck-billed platypus is exhibited for the first time at the Bronx Zoo: "Eats Worm for Lunch," reports the *Times*.

16 SUNDAY
☼ 5:38 AM / 8:25 PM

1907: Actress Barbara Stanwyck is born in Brooklyn.

Jul. 17–23

"There is no air on 5th Avenue, there is nothing but oil & old gasoline & new gasoline—but people who live in New York walk there to get air."

—Edna St. Vincent Millay

17 MONDAY

☼ 5:39 AM / 8:24 PM ● NEW MOON

1763: John Jacob Astor, America's first multimillionaire, is born in Walldorf, in today's Germany.

18 TUESDAY

☼ 5:40 AM / 8:24 PM

Islamic New Year

Matchbox Twenty plays Jones Beach.

19 WEDNESDAY

☼ 5:40 AM / 8:23 PM

1984: New Yorker Geraldine Ferraro is the first woman nominated for vice president by a major party.

20 THURSDAY

☼ 5:41 AM / 8:22 PM

1858: Baseball's first "all-star" game (and the first with paid admission) is played in Queens, a few blocks from today's Citi Field.

21 FRIDAY

☼ 5:42 AM / 8:21 PM

1853: The New York State Legislature sets aside hundreds of acres in Manhattan for Central Park.

22 SATURDAY

☼ 5:43 AM / 8:21 PM

1939: Jane Bolin is sworn in as the first Black female judge in the U.S., in New York City family court.

23 SUNDAY

☼ 5:44 AM / 8:20 PM ♌ LEO

1928: Hubert Selby Jr., author of *Last Exit to Brooklyn* and *Requiem for a Dream*, is born in Brooklyn.

Jul. 24–30

"All the fruit and fruit smells and fruit colors [mix] with the smells of unwashed bodies and perfume and hair grease and liquor and the ... colors of dresses and overalls, and that which dogs like to leave on the sidewalk." —Ralph Ellison

---

24 MONDAY
☼ 5:45 AM / 8:19 PM

1964: Andy Warhol films *Empire*, an 8-hour slow motion film of the Empire State Building, from the 41st floor of the Time-Life Building.

---

25 TUESDAY
☼ 5:46 AM / 8:18 PM ☾ 1ST QUARTER

1841: Mary Rogers, the "Beautiful Cigar Girl," disappears. Her still-unsolved murder inspires Poe's "The Mystery of Marie Roget."

---

26 WEDNESDAY
☼ 5:47 AM / 8:17 PM

1903: The first cross-country automobile trip, which had started from San Francisco on May 25, ends in New York.

---

27 THURSDAY
☼ 5:47 AM / 8:16 PM

1984: *Little Shop of Horrors* opens at the East Village's Orpheum Theatre. It becomes the highest grossing Off Broadway production to that point.

---

28 FRIDAY
☼ 5:48 AM / 8:15 PM

1945: A B-25 bomber accidentally crashes into the 79th floor of the Empire State Building, killing 13 people.

---

29 SATURDAY
☼ 5:49 AM / 8:14 PM

1905: Silent film actress Clara Bow is born in Brooklyn.

---

30 SUNDAY
☼ 5:50 AM / 8:13 PM

1894: Publisher (with her husband Alfred) Blanche Knopf is born on the Upper West Side.

AUGUST

IF YOU THINK JULY IS HOT, welcome to August. When shimmering heat dances up from sidewalks and tar beaches start to melt, take refuge in one of the city's fifty-three public pools. You can spread your towel on the hot concrete at one of the eleven Robert Moses and Mayor LaGuardia opened in the summer of 1938—such as Manhattan's **Highbridge Pool** (in the footprint of an Old Croton Aqueduct reservoir), Brooklyn's **McCarren Park Pool** (once Williamsburg's hippest concert venue), or Queens's **Astoria Pool** (still the city's largest)—don't forget to bring a padlock, and leave your floaties, beach balls, and newspapers at home. Explore the waterways (the so-called sixth borough) on the **South Street Seaport Museum's 1885 schooner** *Pioneer*, or one of the city's newish **ferryboats named by city second graders**, such as the *Ocean Queen Rockstar*, *Lunchbox*, or *McShiny*; or join the **Gowanus Dredgers Canoe Club** to navigate the city's best-known Superfund site (and soon to be luxury neighborhood).

PROFESSOR VATICINATE SAYS, *this month kicks off with some Sun, some cloud, and perhaps thunder loud. Hate to also mention you might get a drenchin'. For August's second week, however, the heavens will smile for a short while. But by midmonth it's back to hot, like it or not—heat indices could top 100. The final week may see a few squalls as the barometer falls.*

NORMALS FOR
CENTRAL PARK
Avg. high: 83.3°
Avg. low: 68.9°
Avg. rainfall: 4.56"

Seventy years ago, this month saw the beginning of the longest heat wave in NYC-weather annals. (A heat wave is defined as when three or more consecutive days hit or exceeds 90°.) August 24, 1953, marked the start of a 12-day heat wave, when the temperature hit 91°. Eleven more brutally hot days followed, with two of those days reaching 100° and 102°.

Sky Watch: The Perseids are the most famous of all meteor showers and tend to provide the majority of meteors seen by nonastronomy enthusiasts. The peak of the shower comes during the predawn hours of the 13th, when those stationed far from city lights will see swift streaks of light darting from the northeast part of the sky. On the 24th at 10:54 p.m., ruddy Antares, one of the brightest and most colorful stars, will slip behind the dark part of the Moon—a stellar eclipse called an "occultation."

ANNALS OF THE NIGHT SKY

The largest meteorite displayed in any museum is the 34-ton Ahnighito meteorite, now exhibited at the Arthur Ross Hall of Meteorites of the American Museum of Natural History. Discovered in 1894 in Greenland, this iron meteorite slammed into Earth some 10,000 years ago.

NYC BOOK OF THE MONTH
Let the Great World Spin by Colum McCann (2009)

The multiple storylines of McCann's novel wind around a startling act of pure beauty—when Philippe Petit walked a highwire between the twin towers of the World Trade Center on August 7, 1974. Like the stories in the book—about Irish brothers, prostitutes, mothers mourning sons lost in Vietnam, and self-important artists—"Everything in New York is built upon another thing" a character notes.

NYC MOVIE OF THE MONTH
Dog Day Afternoon, directed by Sidney Lumet, starring Al Pacino and John Cazale (1975)

This crime drama, which won the Academy Award for Best Screenplay, was based closely on the real-life robbery of a Chase Manhattan branch in Gravesend, Brooklyn, on August 22, 1972. That was indeed a hot day in the city, with temperatures reaching at least 87°.

August has 31 days.

Jul. 31–Aug. 6

"In this metropolis ... there is no public street where the stranger may not go safely ... provided he knows how to mind his own business and is sober."
—Jacob Riis

31 MONDAY

☼ 5:51 AM / 8:12 PM

1904: Sportswriter Arthur Daley, who penned over 10,000 daily columns for the *New York Times*, is born in New York City.

1 TUESDAY

☼ 5:52 AM / 8:11 PM ○ FULL MOON

1945: Congressman Adam Clayton Powell Jr. marries singer and pianist Hazel Scott, with a reception at the integrated Café Society.

2 WEDNESDAY

☼ 5:53 AM / 8:10 PM

1979: *Gilda Radner: Live from New York* opens at the Winter Garden Theater.

3 THURSDAY

☼ 5:54 AM / 8:09 PM

1808: Hamilton Fish (governor of NY, U.S. senator, and secretary of state under Ulysses S. Grant) is born in Greenwich Village.

4 FRIDAY

☼ 5:55 AM / 8:08 PM

1974: Patti Smith performs in Central Park.

5 SATURDAY

☼ 5:56 AM / 8:07 PM

1966: Workers start construction on the World Trade Center "slurry" wall—3 feet thick and 75 feet deep.

6 SUNDAY

☼ 5:57 AM / 8:05 PM

Ecuadorian Day Parade, Jackson Heights, Queens

Aug. 7–13

"If New Yorkers are unflappable, impervious and stoic on the sidewalks, we are raging, delighted, terrified, dancing, sobbing messes in the subway tunnels."
—Qian Julie Wang

7 MONDAY
☼ 5:58 AM / 8:04 PM

1980: John Lennon and Yoko Ono start recording *Double Fantasy* at the Hit Factory in New York.

8 TUESDAY
☼ 5:59 AM / 8:03 PM ◐ 3RD QUARTER

1885: Nearly 250,000 people watch President Ulysses S. Grant's funeral procession.

9 WEDNESDAY
☼ 6:00 AM / 8:02 PM

1928: Basketball star Bob Cousy is born in Manhattan.

10 THURSDAY
☼ 6:01 AM / 8:00 PM

1926: Benjamin Ward, first African American New York City Police Commissioner, is born in Brooklyn.

11 FRIDAY
☼ 6:02 AM / 7:59 PM

1885: Joseph Pulitzer's *New York World* announces that it has raised $102,000 from 120,000 donors to construct the pedestal for the Statue of Liberty.

12 SATURDAY
☼ 6:03 AM / 7:58 PM

1958: Photographer Art Kane gathers 57 jazz musicians for a group portrait on the stoop of 17 East 126th St. for *Esquire* magazine.

13 SUNDAY
☼ 6:04 AM / 7:56 PM

Dominican Day Parade, 6th Ave.

Aug. 14–20

"He stood at the corner of Wall Street.... He noticed the swirls of dust in the cracks of the pavement, the rubbish in the gutters, the ceaseless stream of perspiring faces that poured by under tilted hats."
—Edith Wharton

---

14 MONDAY

☼ 6:05 AM / 7:55 PM

2003: A blackout affecting 8 states plunges NYC into darkness.

---

15 TUESDAY

☼ 6:06 AM / 7:54 PM

1991: Paul Simon performs in Central Park.

---

16 WEDNESDAY

☼ 6:07 AM / 7:52 PM ● NEW MOON

Feast of Saint Rocco

1974: The Ramones play their first gig—at CBGB.

---

17 THURSDAY

☼ 6:08 AM / 7:51 PM

1943: Robert De Niro is born in Greenwich Village.

---

18 FRIDAY

☼ 6:09 AM / 7:49 PM

Kweendom comedy night at Pete's Candy Store

---

19 SATURDAY

☼ 6:10 AM / 7:48 PM

1936: Mayor LaGuardia honors Yankee Lou Gehrig for playing his 1,800th successive game.

---

20 SUNDAY

☼ 6:11 AM / 7:47 PM

1893: 800 anarchists, including Emma Goldman, meet at Covenant Hall, 56 Orchard St.

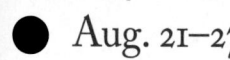

Aug. 21–27

"Is it dirty
does it look dirty
that's what you think of in the city
does it just seem dirty"
—Frank O'Hara

21 MONDAY
☼ 6:12 AM / 7:45 PM

1835: The *Sun* publishes the first part of a series on "Celestial Discoveries" that included poppy-like flowers, bison-like animals, and human-like bats on the moon—and became known as the Great Moon Hoax.

22 TUESDAY
☼ 6:13 AM / 7:44 PM

1989: John F. Kennedy Jr. rides the subway to work on his first day as an assistant district attorney.

23 WEDNESDAY
☼ 6:14 AM / 7:42 PM ♍ VIRGO

1997: The first day of Venus Williams's first U.S. Open at Arthur Ashe Stadium in Queens

24 THURSDAY
☼ 6:15 AM / 7:41 PM ☾ 1ST QUARTER

1893: A hurricane known as the Midnight Storm destroys more than 100 trees in Central Park.

25 FRIDAY
☼ 6:16 AM / 7:39 PM

1876: During construction of the Brooklyn Bridge, mechanic E. F. Farrington crosses the East River in a boatswain's chair suspended on ropes of steel wire stretched across the towers.

26 SATURDAY
☼ 6:17 AM / 7:38 PM

1974: Robert Moses issues a 3,500-word rebuttal to Robert Caro's *The Power Broker*.

27 SUNDAY
☼ 6:18 AM / 7:36 PM

New York Tugboat Race

SEPTEMBER

Labor Day marks the end of summer and for some a comforting return to the routine of the neighborhood. A daily walk or scooter ride to school, a stop for coffee with a favorite barista, or a paper and a bit of gossip picked up at the corner deli—if there's one thing New Yorkers know, it's that *their* neighborhood is the *best* neighborhood. In September, Little Italy's **Feast of San Gennaro** is more than just the chance to eat fried dough and ride a Ferris wheel in the middle of the street—it's a celebration of one of New York's oldest immigrant neighborhoods. The **West Indian American Day Carnival** celebrates Caribbean culture in Brooklyn's Crown Heights, while the borough's oldest Italian Roman Catholic parish honors the **Feast of Our Lady of Sorrows** with a procession through Carroll Gardens—reminders that not everyone who gets tossed into the city's great melting pot comes out the same.

Professor Vaticinate says, *traditionally, Labor Day is a case of summer flew; watch for a few showers and thunder-bumpers. After the holiday, one final round of heat and humidity; kids will hate to go back to school, they'd rather be in the pool. Just in time for the equinox, seasonal quirks: an offshore storm lurks; maybe even a Hurricane Watch (the mull before the storm). September finishes invigorating and chilly.*

Normals for
Central Park
Avg. high: 76.2°
Avg. low: 62.3°
Avg. rainfall: 4.31"

On September 24, 1950, a 200-mile-wide swath of smoke from a series of smoldering fires in the forests of Northern Alberta in Canada cast an awesome pall over the Great Lakes, parts of New York state, and southern New England. The smoke produced an unusual midday darkness and caused the disk of the Sun to shine in eerie hues of pink, blue, and even purple!

Sky Watch: Venus, having transitioned into the morning sky, again attains its maximum brilliance on the 19th, glowing like a beacon in the dawn sky. The Autumnal Equinox occurs at 2:51 a.m. on the 23rd—the official start of fall. On the evening of the 26th, that bright yellow-white "star" floating to the upper left of the Moon is the ringed wonder of the solar system, Saturn. (Rings are visible with a telescope.) The Harvest Moon shines on the 29th.

ANNALS OF THE NIGHT SKY

The seven brightest stars of Ursa Major, the Big Bear, are known as the Big Dipper in the U.S., but in England they are known as the Plough. In 1927, a 13-year-old named Benny Benson won a contest to design a state flag for Alaska. On a blue background he displayed the Dipper and Polaris, the North Star.

NYC BOOK OF THE MONTH
Extremely Loud and Incredibly Close
by Jonathan Safran Foer (2005)

Foer confronts the tragedy of 9/11 through the story of a 9-year-old boy who loses his father in the attack. The child narrator, Oskar, joins a list of fictional precocious city kids from Harriet the Spy to Holden Caulfield. The book is also noteworthy for using photography as a narrative device.

NYC MOVIE OF THE MONTH
The September Issue, directed by R. J. Cutler,
starring Anna Wintour, Grace Coddington,
André Leon Talley, and Hamish Bowles (2009)

Chronicling *Vogue*'s all-important 2007 fall fashion issue—the year's largest—*The September Issue* introduced larger-than-life personalities like Grace Coddington and André Leon Talley to a wider audience. But it also captured a vanishing moment, pre–financial crisis, when lavish print publications were still the magazine industry norm.

September has 30 days.

Aug. 28–Sep. 3

"Cézanne said, 'I love to paint people who have grown old naturally in the country.' And I say I love to paint people who have been torn to shreds by the rat race in New York."
—Alice Neel

28 MONDAY

☼ 6:18 AM / 7:34 PM

The U.S. Open begins at the Billie Jean King National Tennis Center in Queens (through Sep. 10).

29 TUESDAY

☼ 6:19 AM / 7:33 PM

1932: Sherman Billingsley's Stork Club is raided by prohibition agents at its 51st Street location.

30 WEDNESDAY

☼ 6:20 AM / 7:31 PM

1989: Leona Helmsley, "Queen of Mean," is convicted of tax evasion.

31 THURSDAY

☼ 6:21 AM / 7:30 PM
○ FULL MOON

1924: Actor Buddy Hackett is born in Brooklyn.

1 FRIDAY

☼ 6:22 AM / 7:28 PM

1995: Harmony Korine's *Kids* is released.

2 SATURDAY

☼ 6:23 AM / 7:26 PM

Coney Island Beard and Moustache Competition

3 SUNDAY

☼ 6:24 AM / 7:25 PM

Richmond County Fair at Historic Richmond Town, Staten Island (Sep. 2–4)

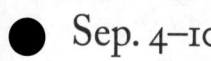

Sep. 4–10

"New York is appalling, fantastically charmless and elaborately dire."
—Henry James

4 MONDAY
☼ 6:25 AM / 7:23 PM

Labor Day

West Indian Carnival (and J'ouvert) in Crown Heights, Brooklyn

5 TUESDAY
☼ 6:26 AM / 7:22 PM

1957: Jack Kerouac's *On the Road* is published by Viking Press.

6 WEDNESDAY
☼ 6:27 AM / 7:20 PM   ☽ 3RD QUARTER

1776: The *American Turtle*, a wooden "submarine," attempts to bomb the British frigate HMS *Eagle*.

7 THURSDAY
☼ 6:28 AM / 7:18 PM

1903: The Federation of American Motorcyclists is organized in New York.

8 FRIDAY
☼ 6:29 AM / 7:17 PM

Coney Island Film Festival (through Sep. 10)

9 SATURDAY
☼ 6:30 AM / 7:15 PM

Bushwig drag festival at the Knockdown Center, Maspeth, Queenz

10 SUNDAY
☼ 6:31 AM / 7:13 PM

Brooklyn's oldest Italian Roman Catholic parish honors the Feast of Our Lady of Sorrows with a procession through Carroll Gardens.

Sep. 11–17

"Here I am, in the great city of New York ... walking amid the hurrying throng, and gazing upon the dazzling wonders of Broadway."
—Frederick Douglass, 1838

11 MONDAY

☼ 6:32 AM / 7:12 PM

Commemoration of the World Trade Center attack at the 9/11 Memorial

12 TUESDAY

☼ 6:33 AM / 7:10 PM

1654: The first Jewish congregation in New York holds its first service.

13 WEDNESDAY

☼ 6:34 AM / 7:08 PM

1899: Henry H. Bliss is struck by a taxicab at West 74th St., becoming the first person to die in a car accident in the U.S.

14 THURSDAY

☼ 6:35 AM / 7:07 PM
● NEW MOON

1928: Labor leader Albert Shanker, president of the UFT, is born on the Lower East Side.

15 FRIDAY

☼ 6:36 AM / 7:05 PM

Rosh Hashana begins.

1905: Photographer Todd Webb is born.

16 SATURDAY

☼ 6:37 AM / 7:03 PM

German-American Steuben Parade, 5th Ave.

17 SUNDAY

☼ 6:38 AM / 7:01 PM

Rosh Hashana ends.

1968: Yves Saint Laurent opens his boutique Rive Gauche on Madison Avenue.

Sep. 18–24

"New York can be seen at her most magical when ... the lighted skyscrapers at night are like sticks of Elizabethan jewelry."
—Cecil Beaton

18 MONDAY
☼ 6:39 AM / 7:00 PM

1851: The first issue of the *New-York Daily Times*, which will become the *New York Times*, is published.

19 TUESDAY
☼ 6:40 AM / 6:58 PM

Feast of San Gennaro

Eric Johnson plays Sony Hall.

20 WEDNESDAY
☼ 6:41 AM / 6:56 PM

1932: An unknown photographer snaps a photo of 11 iron workers eating lunch on a steel beam.

21 THURSDAY
☼ 6:42 AM / 6:55 PM

1960: The *Times* reports that Harlem's Theresa Hotel is "unruffled by its Cuban guests," including Fidel Castro.

22 FRIDAY
☼ 6:43 AM / 6:53 PM ☽ 1ST QUARTER

1776: Patriot and spy Nathan Hale is executed by British soldiers.

23 SATURDAY
☼ 6:44 AM / 6:51 PM ♎ LIBRA

Autumnal Equinox

1962: First Lady Jacqueline Kennedy attends the opening of Philharmonic Hall, the first part of Lincoln Center to open.

24 SUNDAY
☼ 6:45 AM / 6:50 PM

1953: World Heavyweight Champion Rocky Marciano TKOs the hometown favorite, Bronx-born Roland LaStarza, at the Polo Grounds.

Sep. 25–Oct. 1

"We can often be found screaming at strangers in the street but we just as frequently pick them up off the floor."
—Zadie Smith

25 MONDAY
☼ 6:46 AM / 6:48 PM

Yom Kippur

1971: FOOD, an artist-run restaurant at 127 Prince Street opens with free garlic soup and homemade breads.

26 TUESDAY
☼ 6:47 AM / 6:46 PM

1957: Bernstein, Laurents, and Sondheim's *West Side Story* premieres at the Winter Garden Theatre.

27 WEDNESDAY
☼ 6:48 AM / 6:45 PM

2010: The EPA designates Newtown Creek a Superfund site.

28 THURSDAY
☼ 6:49 AM / 6:45 PM
○ FULL MOON

1951: Allie Reynolds of the Yankees has his second no-hitter of the year, and his team clinches the pennant.

29 FRIDAY
☼ 6:50 AM / 6:41 PM

Sukkot begins.

2001: Gilbert Gottfried tells a 9½ minute version of "the Aristocrats"—the dirtiest joke ever—at a Friar's Club roast of Hugh Heffner.

30 SATURDAY
☼ 6:51 AM / 6:40 PM

Brooklyn Book Festival Children's Day in Downtown Brooklyn

1 SUNDAY
☼ 6:52 AM / 6:38 PM

Brooklyn Book Festival and Literary Marketplace in Downtown Brooklyn

OCTOBER

Jack-o-lanterns impaled on wrought-iron fence spikes, skeletons scaling brownstone facades, giant spiders weaving webs over stoops and sidewalks—as Halloween nears, New Yorkers from Striver's Row to East 78th Street to Fort Greene relish the chance to create dioramas of horror for the delight, and sometimes disgust, of trick-or-treaters and passersby alike. Costume stores pop up, zombie-like, in otherwise abandoned storefronts, and the ghosts of Old New York get restless. You might encounter Gertrude Tredwell, who died in 1933 in the same bed where she was born, roaming the **Merchant's House Museum**—or you might see a few specters during one of **Green-Wood Cemetery's Late October tours**. Pick pumpkins at **Historic Richmond Town's Decker Farm**, celebrate Red Hook's resilience with the 10th annual **Barnacle Parade** on the anniversary of Hurricane Sandy, and indulge in a different kind of spirits at the New York City Wine and Food Festival.

Professor Vaticinate says, *this month starts with days of gold, but it's too cold. Showers will follow. Skies clear and it turns even colder for Columbus Day weekend. Perfect days for leaf peepers north of NYC through midmonth; pleasant temperature days. It's a final fling until next spring. The 24th–27th will be soggy . . . even foggy. Dry but very chilly for Halloween. Boo!*

Normals for Central Park	
Avg. high: 64.5°	Why does the number of clear days reach its annual maximum in October? Chiefly because the greatest prevalence of fair skies in the U.S. is located over West Virginia, where migrating domes of high pressure from the west tend to stall and spread out, producing long spells of fine, dry, and mild weather.
Avg. low: 51.4°	
Avg. rainfall: 4.38"	
Avg. snowfall: 0.1"	

October is the clearest month: 12 days average less than 3/10 cloud cover.

Sky Watch: The 14th will afford us a view of a partial eclipse of the Sun from 12:08 p.m. to 2:36 p.m. Maximum eclipse will come at 1:22 p.m., but only 23 percent of the Sun will be hidden by the passing New Moon; it will appear as if a big bite was taken out of the lower right part of the Sun's disk. (Never look directly at the Sun! For safe viewing methods, refer to *Sky and Telescope* magazine's online guide "How to Safely See a Partial Solar Eclipse.") Jupiter is to the lower right of a waning gibbous Moon late on the night of the 1st and to the lower left of the Hunter's Full Moon on the 28th.

ANNALS OF THE NIGHT SKY

Venus takes 225 days to circle the Sun, but 243 days to make one full turn on its axis—backwards! Hence, a day on Venus is longer than its year. Because of Venus's perpetual cloud cover, we would never see the Sun, but if we could, it would appear to rise in the west and set in the east.

NYC BOOK OF THE MONTH
Native Speaker by Chang-Rae Lee (1995)

Lee's narrator, Henry Park, is the son of Korean immigrants whose job is to spy on the mayoral campaign of another Korean American—a city councilman from Queens. Park struggles with language, culture, and identity, but "still I love it here," he says, "I love the brief Queens sunlight at the end of the day, the warm lamp always reaching through the westward tops of that magnificent city."

NYC MOVIE OF THE MONTH
Breakfast at Tiffany's, directed by Blake Edwards, starring Audrey Hepburn and George Peppard (1961)

Audrey Hepburn steps out of a yellow cab in a black evening gown, croissant in black-gloved hand, and peers into the windows of Tiffany's on Fifth Avenue. This classic moment in NYC filmmaking was shot at 5 a.m., October 8, 1960.

October has 31 days.

Oct. 2–8

"Manhattan is an accumulation of possible disasters that never happen."
—Rem Koolhaas

2 MONDAY
☼ 6:53 AM / 6:36 PM

1932: The Yankees win their 12th consecutive World Series game—sweeping the series for the third time.

3 TUESDAY
☼ 6:54 AM / 6:35 PM

1934: The Rainbow Room opens at Rockefeller Center.

4 WEDNESDAY
☼ 6:55 AM / 6:33 PM

1946: Actress and activist Susan Sarandon is born in Jackson Heights, Queens.

5 THURSDAY
☼ 6:56 AM / 6:31 PM

1977: President Carter tours Charlotte Street in the South Bronx.

6 FRIDAY
☼ 6:57 AM / 6:30 PM   ☽ 3RD QUARTER

Sukkot ends.

1959: Rock Hudson brings Tallulah Bankhead to the premiere of *Pillow Talk* at the Palace Theater.

7 SATURDAY
☼ 6:58 AM / 6:28 PM

New York City Comic Con (through Oct. 10)

8 SUNDAY
☼ 6:59 AM / 6:26 PM

Harvest Festival at the Vander Ende–Onderdonk House in Ridgewood, Queens

Oct. 9–15

"New York at its best, on a shiny, blue-and-white autumn day with its buildings cut diagonally in halves of light and shadow, with its straight, neat avenues colored with quick throngs, like confetti in a breeze" —Dorothy Parker

---

9 MONDAY
☿ 7:00 AM / 6:25 PM

Columbus Day • Indigenous People's Day

Columbus Day Parade on 5th Ave.

Indigenous People's Day activities at the National Museum of the American Indian

---

10 TUESDAY
☿ 7:01 AM / 6:23 PM

1948: The Little Church around the Corner (1 East 29th St.) celebrates its 100th birthday.

---

11 WEDNESDAY
☿ 7:02 AM / 6:22 PM

1984: August Wilson's *Ma Rainey's Black Bottom* premieres at the Cort Theater.

---

12 THURSDAY
☿ 7:03 AM / 6:20 PM

New York City Food & Wine Festival opens.

---

13 FRIDAY
☿ 7:04 AM / 6:19 PM

Dream Theater with special guest Arch Echo play Kings Theater, Brooklyn.

---

14 SATURDAY
☿ 7:04 AM / 6:17 PM ● NEW MOON

Total solar eclipse begins at 11:03 AM (ends 4:55 PM).

Open House New York Weekend (and 15th)

---

15 SUNDAY
☿ 7:06 AM / 6:16 PM

1969: Mayor Lindsay addresses demonstrators at the Moratorium to End the War in Vietnam at Bryant Park.

Oct. 16–22

"Money talks and bullshit walks in New York. In a lot of cities, probably—but here, the nation's shrine to unrestricted predatory capitalism, money has nearly talismanic power."

—N. K. Jemisin

16 MONDAY
☼ 7:08 AM / 6:14 PM

1893: Anarchist Emma Goldman is sentenced to a year in prison following a Union Square rally of unemployed women.

17 TUESDAY
☼ 7:09 AM / 6:13 PM

1956: 13-year-old Bobby Fischer beats Donald Byrne in "The Chess Game of the Century" at Marshall Chess Club in Greenwich Village.

18 WEDNESDAY
☼ 7:10 AM / 6:11 PM

1985: Nintendo releases a limited number of Nintendo Entertainment Systems for sale in New York City.

19 THURSDAY
☼ 7:11 AM / 6:10 PM

1943: *Othello*, starring Paul Robeson in the title role, opens at the Schubert.

20 FRIDAY
☼ 7:12 AM / 6:08 PM

Brooklyn Folk Festival, St. Ann's Church (through Oct. 22)

21 SATURDAY
☼ 7:13 AM / 6:07 PM   ◐ 1ST QUARTER

Pumpkin picking at Historic Richmond Town's Decker Farm (Sat. & Sun. through Oct.)

22 SUNDAY
☼ 7:14 AM / 6:05 PM

1903: Actor Jerome Horwitz, better known as Curly (of Larry, Curly, and Moe) is born in Brooklyn.

Oct. 23–29

"The lazy are excited by the perpetual motion of the busy, or at least compelled to bestir themselves to avoid being run over."
—Theodore Dwight, 1833

23 MONDAY

☼ 7:15 AM / 6:04 PM ♏ SCORPIO

1963: Neil Simon's *Barefoot in the Park* opens at the Biltmore Theater.

24 TUESDAY

☼ 7:16 AM / 6:02 PM

1931: 30,000 guests attend the dedication of the George Washington Bridge.

25 WEDNESDAY

☼ 7:18 AM / 6:01 PM

1957: Crime boss Albert Anastasia, who controlled New York City's waterfront, is murdered in a barber's chair at the Park Sheraton Hotel on 56th St. and 7th Ave.

26 THURSDAY

☼ 7:19 AM / 6:00 PM   ●

1825: Erie Canal opens, connecting the Great Lakes with the Atlantic Ocean via the Hudson River.

27 FRIDAY

☼ 7:20 AM / 5:58 PM

1787: The first of the Federalist Papers by Alexander Hamilton, James Madison, and John Jay is published in the New York *Independent Journal*.

28 SATURDAY

☼ 7:21 AM / 5:57 PM   ○ FULL MOON

1983: Principal photography for *Ghostbusters* begins in New York.

29 SUNDAY

☼ 7:22 AM / 5:56 PM

The 10th annual Barnacle Parade celebrates the resilience of Red Hook, Brooklyn, on the anniversary of Hurricane Sandy.

NOVEMBER

New Yorkers' passion for theater runs deep, from 1798, when the 2,000-seat Park Theatre opened downtown, to just after 9/11, when Broadway stars such as Patti LuPone and Nathan Lane filled Duffy Square with the sound of Kander and Ebb's "New York, New York." Not even a pandemic could keep New Yorkers away for long. By November the **fall theater season** is underway. Savvy theatergoers skip the fees from online ticket brokers by heading straight to the box office, waiting it out on the sidewalk for rush tickets, or trying their luck with digital ticket lotteries. There's nothing wrong with grabbing a good old-fashioned preshow bite on Restaurant Row—especially if holiday visitors are in tow. Bring your guests to see the **Macy's Thanksgiving Day Parade** balloons being blown up by the American Museum of Natural History, or the **Rockefeller Tree lighting,** or take them **off-Broadway** for the black box, experimental, possibly baffling experience they just can't get in Kansas.

Professor Vaticinate says, *at the start of the month the barometer will be dropping . . . and it will be sopping. Then come dry and chilly conditions, great for the marathon! During the second week, showers will return, but temps will be mild. Around the 20th, batten down the hatches; wind- and rain-whipped trees are stripped. Even a few flakes might mix in. For Thanksgiving there's a movement for improvement, but November could end with sleet or wet snow.*

Normals for
Central Park
Avg. high: 54.0°
Avg. low: 42.0°
Avg. rainfall: 3.58"
Avg. snowfall: 0.5"

NYC endured an unusually polluted atmosphere in late November 1966. The tristate area saw carbon dioxide levels rise from 8 parts per million on the 22nd to 35 ppm on the 24th. Oxides of nitrogen, sulfur, and hydrocarbons also showed maximums. An increase of 24 deaths per day was reported during this period.

Sky Watch: On the 9th, be sure to set your alarm clock for 5 a.m. and then head outside to a location with an unobstructed view toward the east-northeast to see the most spectacular Venus/Moon pairing of 2023. You'll likely also see the dark of the crescent Moon eerily glowing with a blue-gray cast, a phenomenon known as "Earthshine." Saturn sits to the upper right of a Half Moon on the 20th. During the overnight hours of the 24th–25th, watch the waxing gibbous Moon slowly creep toward Jupiter.

ANNALS OF THE NIGHT SKY

Did you know that from the surface of the planet Mercury the Sun can briefly appear to stop and reverse its course across the sky? When that rocky world reaches the point in its orbit closest to the Sun, for a period spanning eight days the Sun appears to slow down in its westward track across the sky, halt, and then turn back toward the east.

NYC BOOK OF THE MONTH
The Street by Ann Petry (1946)

Ann Petry's heartbreaking novel of a single mother striving, and failing, to provide a safe home for her son on 116th Street opens with an evocative description of the November wind whipping around pedestrians: "And then the wind grabbed their hats, pried their scarves from around their necks, stuck its fingers inside their coat collars, blew their coats away from their bodies."

NYC MOVIE OF THE MONTH
Moonstruck, directed by Norman Jewison, starring Cher and Nicholas Cage (1987)

Cher falls for her boring fiancé's passionate younger brother in this quirky story of family, infidelity, and the opera set in brownstone Brooklyn under an enormous full moon. Locations include the family house, at 19 Cranberry Street in Brooklyn Heights, a bakery at Henry and Sackett Streets in Cobble Hill, and the wintry plaza at Lincoln Center.

November has 30 days.

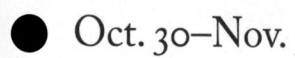

Oct. 30–Nov. 5

"The New York Decathlon would consist of four events . . . since everyone in New York is very busy. . . . The four events would be Press Agentry, Dry Cleaning and Laundering, Party-going, and Dog-owning." —Fran Lebowitz

30 MONDAY
☼ 7:23 AM / 5:55 PM

Last chance to see *Shrine Room Projects: Rohini Devashet/Palden Weinreb* at the Rubin Museum

31 TUESDAY
☼ 7:24 AM / 5:53 PM

Halloween

Greenwich Village Halloween Parade

1 WEDNESDAY
☼ 7:26 AM / 5:52 PM

1939: John D. Rockefeller Jr. installs the ceremonial final rivet to complete Rockefeller Center.

2 THURSDAY
☼ 7:27 AM / 5:51 PM

1907: J. P. Morgan invites bankers to his library to formulate a plan to stop the Panic of 1907.

3 FRIDAY
☼ 7:28 AM / 5:50 PM

2014: One World Trade Center opens.

4 SATURDAY
☼ 7:29 AM / 5:49 PM

1964: Comedian Lenny Bruce and Café Au Go Go club owner Howard Solomon are found guilty of obscenity.

5 SUNDAY
☼ 6:30 AM / 4:47 PM ☽ 3RD QUARTER

Daylight saving time ends.

New York City Marathon

Nov. 6–12

"Like sap at the first frost, at five o'clock men and women begin to drain gradually out of the tall buildings downtown, grayfaced throngs flood subways and tubes, vanish underground."
—John Dos Passos

6 MONDAY
☼ 6:31 AM / 4:46 PM

New York Comedy Festival (through Nov. 12)

7 TUESDAY
☼ 6:33 AM / 4:45 PM

Election Day

1938: Rockefeller Center opens the "Sidewalk Superintendent's Club," an area from which to view the construction of the complex.

8 WEDNESDAY
☼ 6:34 AM / 4:44 PM

1929: The Museum of Modern Art opens with a show of Cézanne, Gauguin, Seurat, and Van Gogh at the Heckscher Building, 5th Ave. and 42nd St.

9 THURSDAY
☼ 6:35 AM / 4:43 PM

1965: One of the biggest power failures in U.S. history traps 800,000 commuters in the subway.

10 FRIDAY
☼ 6:36 AM / 4:42 PM

2005: Fulton Fish Market's last night at Fulton Street in Lower Manhattan

11 SATURDAY
☼ 6:37 AM / 4:41 PM

Veterans Day

1997: Green Day trashes Tower Records' flagship location on Broadway during an in-store performance.

12 SUNDAY
☼ 6:39 AM / 4:40 PM

Diwali/Deepavali

1967: Pink Floyd appears in New York City for the first time, at the Cheetah Club.

Nov. 13–19

"The theater here is something to wonder at.... Everybody [says] their lines at such a rate you'd think you wouldn't understand a word—but you do! And then it ... struck me—that's the way people actually talk!" —Noel Coward

13 MONDAY
☼ 6:40 AM / 4:40 PM ● NEW MOON

1927: The Holland Tunnel opens for automobiles.

14 TUESDAY
☼ 6:41 AM / 4:39 PM

1943: Leonard Bernstein makes his conducting debut for the New York Philharmonic at Carnegie Hall, filling in for Bruno Walter.

15 WEDNESDAY
☼ 6:42 AM / 4:389 PM

1956: Elvis's first film, *Love Me Tender*, premieres at the Paramount Theater.

16 THURSDAY
☼ 6:43 AM / 4:37 PM

1926: The New York Rangers play their first hockey game.

17 FRIDAY
☼ 6:44 AM / 4:36 PM

1920: Harlem's Apollo Theater opens.

18 SATURDAY
☼ 6:46 AM / 4:35 PM

The Holiday Train Show opens at the New York Botanical Garden.

19 SUNDAY
☼ 6:47 AM / 4:35 PM

1933: Larry King is born in New York City.

Nov. 20–26

"You are a New Yorker when what was there before is more real and solid than what is here now."
—Colson Whitehead

20 MONDAY

☼ 6:48 AM / 4:34 PM ☾ 1ST QUARTER

1966: Kander and Ebb's *Cabaret*, starring Joel Grey as Master of Ceremonies, premieres at the Broadhurst Theatre.

21 TUESDAY

☼ 6:49 AM / 4:33 PM

1934: *Anything Goes*, with music by Cole Porter, debuts at the Alvin Theatre.

22 WEDNESDAY

☼ 6:50 AM / 4:33 PM ♐ SAGITTARIUS

Macy's Thanksgiving Day Parade balloons inflated on Columbus Ave. between 77th and 81st Sts.

23 THURSDAY

☼ 6:51 AM / 4:32 PM

Thanksgiving Day
Macy's Thanksgiving Day Parade

24 FRIDAY

☼ 6:52 AM / 4:32 PM

Native American Heritage Day

1986: Susan Sontag's "The Way We Live Now" is published in the *New Yorker*.

25 SATURDAY

☼ 6:54 AM / 4:31 PM

1865: Six Confederate officers try, and fail, to burn down New York City. "Do you suppose New York thieves would have bungled the business so stupidly?" asks the *New York World*.

26 SUNDAY

☼ 6:55 AM / 4:31 PM

1961: Casey Stengel rides a "Meet the Mets" float in the Macy's Thanksgiving Day Parade to introduce the city's new team.

DECEMBER

WITH THE SLOW-MOVING TOURISTS, puffer coat–piercing wind, and shockingly deep puddles of icy black slush, leaving the apartment during December is hard. But **brightly lit holiday trees** from Midtown to East Harlem to Sunset Park can make your commute home in the inky darkness of five o'clock a little bit more cheerful. And when the banging, tapping, hissing squeal of the radiator chases you out of your apartment, why not give in and go see the magical **holiday windows on Fifth Avenue**. Nothing can replace the irreverent nonchalance of Barneys' best windows, but the glittering jewel boxes of Saks, Tiffany's, and especially Bergdorf's might just chase away the holiday blues—even better if you bring a child. While you're at it, you might as well trudge to the eighth floor of Macy's to see the great big man in the red suit, and his many helpers (Entrance Elf, Photo Elf, Elevator Elf) at **Santaland**—or maybe head to a cozy pub or chalet-themed rooftop bar instead.

PROFESSOR VATICINATE SAYS, *science says the climate's warming, but every winter it's storming! Case in point: December opens with wind, snows, and rains—a torrent, we warrant. Tranquil weather will favor holiday shoppers from the 8th through the 15th. Then, a corker of a storm as holiday plans form. But don't despair, drier air will pave the way for Santa's sleigh: fair and clear for holiday cheer. The year ends as it began, though: wet! So, "wring" out the old.*

NORMALS FOR
CENTRAL PARK
Avg. high: 44.3°
Avg. low: 33.8°
Avg. rainfall: 4.38"
Avg. snowfall: 4.9"

Fifty years ago, on December 16–17, 1973, the tristate area was subjected to one of the most damaging ice storms in history, resulting in power losses to millions. In Connecticut, the storm was described as the worst ice storm in history, with damage to trees greater than that of the September 1938 hurricane.

Sky Watch: The Geminid meteor shower—the year's very best—peaks during the overnight hours of the 14th–15th. From a location far from bright lights, after 9 p.m. you'll likely spy many "shooting stars" emanating from out of the northeast sky. Be sure to bundle up! Venus and the Moon pair off again at dawn on the 9th. Saturn hovers above the Moon on the evening of the 17th. Winter arrives on the 21st at 10:27 p.m.

ANNALS OF THE NIGHT SKY

Fifty years ago, on December 28, 1973, sky watchers worldwide were straining to get a look at Comet Kohoutek, billed as the "Comet of the Century"—possibly to be visible even in daytime. Instead, it ended up shining far dimmer than forecast, and ending up being branded the "Flop of the Century."

NYC BOOK OF THE MONTH
The Catcher in the Rye by J. D. Salinger (1951)

Angst-ridden Holden Caulfield flunks out of prep school just before Christmas break and spends three days wandering around the post–WWII city—a bar in Greenwich village, an encounter with a prostitute and her pimp, the Museum of Natural History, even ice-skating at Rockefeller Center. The book is one of the most challenged in U.S. literature—and a touchstone for a certain kind of brainy, rebellious teenager.

NYC MOVIE OF THE MONTH
When Harry Met Sally, directed by Rob Reiner, starring Meg Ryan and Billy Crystal (1989)

The enduring appeal of this quintessential romantic comedy (which lodged Meg Ryan in American hearts) lies in the way writer Nora Ephron's New York-y attitude pierces the cloying sentimentality. Memorable scenes filmed on location in Manhattan—in Washington Square Park, Katz's Deli, Central Park, the Met's Temple of Dendur, and the Puck Building on New Year's Eve—make the city seem just as romantic as the plot.

December has 31 days.

Nov. 27–Dec. 3

"New York does nothing for those of us who are inclined to love her except implant in our hearts a homesickness that baffles us."
—Maeve Brennan

27 MONDAY
☼ 6:56 AM / 4:30 PM   ○ FULL MOON

1911: British suffragist Emmeline Pankhurst addresses a large crowd on Wall Street.

28 TUESDAY
☼ 6:57 AM / 4:30 PM

1974: John Lennon makes his last concert appearance, joining Elton John onstage at Madison Square Garden.

29 WEDNESDAY
☼ 6:58 AM / 4:29 PM

Rockefeller Center Christmas Tree Lighting

30 THURSDAY
☼ 6:59 AM / 4:29 PM

1979: Norman Mailer attends a rally in support of Pete Hamill, who had just been fired by the *Daily News* for being "far, far to the left of The News' readership."

1 FRIDAY
☼ 7:00 AM / 4:29 PM

1980: Paloma Picasso introduces her jewelry collection at Tiffany & Co.

2 SATURDAY
☼ 7:01 AM / 4:29 PM

1923: Soprano Maria Callas is born in Manhattan.

3 SUNDAY
☼ 7:02 AM / 4:28 PM

1979: Debbie Harry attends the opening of *Fashions of the Hapsburg Era* at the Metropolitan Museum of Art.

Dec. 4–10

"I gaze with a thousand eyes and listen with a thousand ears all through the day. . . . New York is not a place where one finds rest. But did I come here for rest?"
—Kahlil Gibran

4 MONDAY

☼ 7:03 AM / 4:28 PM

1909: The *New York Amsterdam News* is founded.

5 TUESDAY

☼ 7:04 AM / 4:28 PM ☽ 3RD QUARTER

1954: Eartha Kitt performs on Ed Sullivan's *Toast of the Town*.

6 WEDNESDAY

☼ 7:05 AM / 4:28 PM

1966: Timothy Leary's multimedia presentation *Illumination of the Buddha* is performed at the Village Theatre.

7 THURSDAY

☼ 7:06 AM / 4:28 PM

Hanukkah begins.

Pearl Harbor Remembrance Day

1988: President Reagan and Vice President Bush meet with Mikhail Gorbachev on Governor's Island.

8 FRIDAY

☼ 7:07 AM / 4:28 PM

1981: The New York City Gay Men's Chorus performs at Carnegie Hall, making them the first openly gay musical group to do so.

9 SATURDAY

☼ 7:08 AM / 4:28 PM

1985: The NYC Dept. of Health closes the New St. Marks Baths, a gay bathhouse at the time the largest of its kind in the world.

10 SUNDAY

☼ 7:08 AM / 4:28 PM

1896: The New York Aquarium opens in Castle Garden, Battery Park.

Dec. 11–17

"New York blazes like a magnificent jewel in its fit setting of sea, and earth, and stars."
—Thomas Wolfe

11 MONDAY
☼ 7:09 AM / 4:28 PM

1964: Che Guevara delivers his speech "Patria O Muerte" at the UN General Assembly.

12 TUESDAY
☼ 7:10 AM / 4:28 PM ● NEW MOON

1966: Joan Rivers performs on the Ed Sullivan show.

13 WEDNESDAY
☼ 7:11 AM / 4:28 PM

1957: Steve Buscemi is born in New York City.

14 THURSDAY
☼ 7:12 AM / 4:29 PM

1978: Billy Joel plays Madison Square Garden for the first time.

15 FRIDAY
☼ 7:12 AM / 4:29 PM

Hanukkah ends.

1949: Birdland Jazz Club opens at 1678 Broadway, near 52nd St.

16 SATURDAY
☼ 7:13 AM / 4:29 PM

1962: Barbara Streisand appears on the Ed Sullivan show for the first time.

17 SUNDAY
☼ 7:14 AM / 4:30 PM

1904: Artist Paul Cadmus is born in Manhattan. Both of his parents were visual artists as well.

Dec. 18–24

"You must believe in it all: in Rock Center and the Flatiron Building and Cooper Union and even Trump Tower ... that the women are the prettiest, the water the purest, and the taxi drivers the friendliest." —Noel Behn

18 MONDAY

☼ 7:14 AM / 4:30 PM

1981: The *Times* announces the end of a 17-day strike by private sanitation workers, who promise to pick up 100,000 tons of garbage as a Christmas present to New Yorkers.

19 TUESDAY

☼ 7:15 AM / 4:30 PM ☽ 1ST QUARTER

1945: Dorothy Shaver is named president of Lord & Taylor. She is the first female executive of a department store.

20 WEDNESDAY

☼ 7:15 AM / 4:31 PM

1955: The first full-scale model of a man-made satellite goes on view at the American Museum of Natural History's Hayden Planetarium.

21 THURSDAY

☼ 7:16 AM / 4:31 PM

Winter Solstice

1964: Jackie Robinson and cofounders open the Black-owned Freedom National Bank in Harlem.

22 FRIDAY

☼ 7:16 AM / 4:32 PM ♑ CAPRICORN

Michael Wavves plays the Mercury Lounge.

23 SATURDAY

☼ 7:17 AM / 4:32 PM

2003: Governor Pataki grants a posthumous pardon to Lenny Bruce for his 1964 obscenity conviction.

24 SUNDAY

☼ 7:17 AM / 4:33 PM

Christmas Eve

Last chance to see the Christmas Spectacular Starring the Radio City Rockettes at Radio City Music Hall before Christmas

Dec. 25–31

"In the end, the only thing the true New Yorker knows about New York is that is it unknowable."
—Pete Hamill

25 MONDAY
☼ 7:18 AM / 4:33 PM

Christmas Day

Eat at a Chinese restaurant.

26 TUESDAY
☼ 7:18 AM / 4:34 PM   ○ FULL MOON

Kwanzaa begins.

1978: Frank Zappa records a series of shows (through Dec. 29) at the Palladium for the album *Zappa in New York*.

27 WEDNESDAY
☼ 7:18 AM / 4:35 PM

1932: 6,200 people, including Al Smith, Amelia Earhart, and John D. Rockefeller Jr., attend the opening night of Radio City Music Hall.

28 THURSDAY
☼ 7:19 AM / 4:35 PM

1967: Muriel Siebert buys her seat on the New York Stock Exchange—the first woman to do so.

29 FRIDAY
☼ 7:19 AM / 4:36 PM

Off Peak, Yard Sale play the Mercury Lounge.

30 SATURDAY
☼ 7:19 AM / 4:37 PM

1873: Al Smith is born in the Fourth Ward on the Lower East Side.

31 SUNDAY
☼ 7:19 AM / 4:38 PM

New Year's Eve

Times Square Ball Drop

New York Road Runners Midnight Run

Contributors

GENERAL EDITOR Susan Gail Johnson is a museum consultant, editor, and content developer with a special expertise in New York City. She managed numerous major exhibitions and publications for the Museum of the City of New York and served as project director of its institution-defining permanent exhibition, *New York at Its Core*. Johnson holds a master's degree from NYU's John W. Draper Interdisciplinary Program in Humanities and Social Thought.

ASTRONOMER Joe Rao is an Associate and Guest Lecturer at the Hayden Planetarium of the American Museum of Natural History, astronomy columnist for *Natural History* magazine, Night Sky columnist for Space.com, and a contributing editor at *Sky and Telescope* magazine.

METEOROLOGIST Professor Vaticinate is the *nom de plume* of an experienced professional meteorologist.

FASHION FORECASTER Raissa Bretaña is a New York–based fashion historian and adjunct instructor at the Fashion Institute of Technology. She also hosts a popular video series for *Glamour*.

ILLUSTRATOR Andrey Kokorin's work has appeared in magazines, advertisements, and product packaging around the world.

Compilation copyright © 2023 Abbeville Press. All rights reserved under international copyright conventions. No part of this publication may be reproduced or utilized in any form or by any means, electronic or mechanical, including photocopying, recording, or by any information retrieval system, without permission in writing from the publisher. Inquiries should be addressed to Abbeville Press, 655 Third Avenue, New York, NY 10017. The text of this almanac was set in Caslon Pro. Printed in Turkey.

ISBN 978-0-7892-5462-7

Second edition

1 3 5 7 9 10 8 6 4 2

This almanac is published by Abbeville Press, www.abbeville.com.
For bulk and premium sales, call 1-800-ARTBOOK.
Customized covers and complimentary point-of-sale displays
are available with bulk orders of the almanac.